Confessions of An HR Pro:

Stories of Defeat & Triumph

ISBN: 978-0-578-90582-2 (Paperback)
Self-Published

Any references to historical events, real people, or real places are used fictitiously. Names, characters, and places are products of the author's imagination.

Front cover image designed by HR@Heart Consulting Inc.
Book design by HR@Heart Consulting Inc.

First printing edition 2021.

Disclaimer
Considerable care has been taken to ensure this document is both accurate and relevant. However, the author provides no guarantees concerning the accuracy, completeness or relevance of the contents of this book to your organization.

https://hratheart.co/

Confessions of An HR Pro:

Stories of Defeat & Triumph

Julie Turney

Feedback from my HR community on LinkedIn:

"HR usually puts themselves last on the list in the organization. So busy outing fires and supporting, we forget we need support too. Keep sharing, Julie. You are needed more now than ever."
Charlene Pedro – HR Consultant – Conventus Consult Inc.

"It wasn't until I had chest pains and was in the ER that I realized I was burnout and STRESSED! I had to leave that company to save my own life. Since then, self-care is an everyday focus for me."
Felicia J. Felton - Visionary Senior-Level Human Resources Leader

"Throughout this pandemic, I've had employees tell me that I can't be down because they need me to bring joy and positivity. But you're right; you can't pour from an empty cup. I try, but I'm human too."
Tracey Carter – Director of Human Resources

"When we have workplace issues, sometimes with our boss who could be the CEO or head of HR, who do we go to? We don't... we shut up and colour, and eventually, the stress is too much for some."
Emily Woloshin, PHR

"I've been at companies where they look for ways to engage everyone BUT HR! Good looking out for HR people- we need more of that now more than ever."
Erin Sullivan-Lopez – Talent Development Business Partner

Dedication

To Daddy

I wish you could see this part of my journey. I miss you terribly.

To Almina

I respect your hustle. Thank you, mummy, for showing me all day, every day, how to model a great work ethic.

To Ricardo, Joshua & Jasmin

You are the reasons I strive to do and be better every day. Mummy loves you all so much.

To Rondell

Thank you for holding me accountable at the end and for shouting out, "Holy crap, my wife wrote a book!"

To Angela & Uncle G

This journey all started from conversations with you. Thank you both for believing in me.

To Kianna & Miracle-Ann

Thank you for your support and for being there from day one.

To every HR Pro feeling alone, undervalued, and misunderstood. I see you.

Foreward

In a world where the return on investment measures success, no investment will pay you back more when you treat people with the respect and dignity they deserve.

In a space where all the noise is about how and what HR needs to give (to employees, to managers, to the CEO, to clients, vendors, and so on), Confessions of an HR Pro is about giving back to HR professionals. Giving back recognition, support, hope, belief, and an opportunity for introspection allows us to grow as people and in our work lives.

Reading the confessions and experiences in this book took me on a journey of deep reflection. It confirmed that being a successful HR professional goes beyond 'time to hire' and 'retention rates'. It also goes beyond competencies and skills. Being a successful HR professional means knowing ourselves, becoming aware of how we impact others and relate to them. It is discovering the heart of who we are and perhaps rediscovering the love for our jobs.

This inspiring and helpful book is equal parts insightful and hopeful, confessional and forward-looking, with plenty of glimpses into the past and the lessons learned. No matter where you are in your journey, seasoned or just beginning, Julie and the other HR Pros' share their own first-hand experiences, stories and perspectives on the importance of putting people over processes and creating workplaces where the business is thriving because the people are thriving.

I have known Julie for a few years since we met at an Agile HR training course in London and shared our hopes for the future of HR. Julie left a distinct impression on me as someone who feels compelled to change the future of the world we work in.

In these past two years, Julie has launched her own business helping HR professionals lead with purpose; created her own podcast, "HR Sound Off", to demystify the people in our profession; spoken at global conferences, and facilitated panel discussions about the future direction HR is headed in, and regularly shares her tremendous knowledge and insights via wonderfully crafted blogs and articles.

Publishing a book for all HR people out there who work very hard, letting us know that we are heard, seen, and appreciated, sums up Julie beautifully. Giving, open, supportive, fun and funny, kind and strong, Julie is a brilliant human being and friend. An advocate for a people-focused approach, Julie wants to change the perception of HR from being paper pushers to strategic partners who understand the business needs and the people to create great services and products.

HR is best placed to help companies be successful and shape their futures. What better time to launch a book that seeks to support and empower HR professionals to lead change differently and purposefully by learning from other professionals' actual experiences.

This is a behind the scenes book, written by HR Pros for HR Pros. A book full of never shared before real stories of defeats and triumphs by HR professionals who hope that by opening up about their mistakes and their lessons learned, they are helping others be better prepared and better equipped for whatever comes their way.

Rishita Jones MCIPD

Founder of NRG-HR Strategic Consultancy Services, Amsterdam

Acknowledgements

Sometimes people come into your life at just the right time. There are some fantastic people that I need to acknowledge at this time for whom, without them, I could not have created this book:

Maria Rowe – Thank you for keeping me honest and holding me accountable to my deadlines, despite your busy schedule.

Aura Telman – Thank you for being such a great friend. I will forever cherish our friendship.

Rishita Jones – You are such an inspiration, and I thank you for your support.

Katrina Collier – Thank you for trusting me with your story and for being such a wonderful human being.

Erich Kurschat – My introvert twin, you are the best!

Michelle Strasburger – Thank you for being so willing to share your story. I appreciate you.

Meighan Newhouse – My friend, you are such a blessing to my life. Thank you for always being there.

Perry Timms – I am in constant awe at your ability to give, despite your hectic schedule and commitments. Thank you for saying yes and coming through.

Wendy Dailey – Thank you for sharing your story; you are a true inspiration.

You all said yes to embarking on this journey with me. No matter what, I am forever grateful for all that you have done to get this completed.

CONTENTS

Introduction

"These are my confessions."

Confessions ~ Usher

I experienced my first termination at the age of 22. I was in the third trimester of my pregnancy, and in my heart of hearts, I knew the way they dismissed me could not have been correct. I made a promise from that moment that I would be a better leader when given the opportunity to lead a team.

In my 15+ years as an HR professional, I have often experienced frustration, feeling the need to sit in the proverbial naughty corner before saying something to someone I will eternally regret. To the moments when I felt such pride and joy to be a part of a profession that gets to see people develop and grow to become the person I always knew they could be.

Have you ever seen something in someone that they did not see in themselves? How did it make you feel? What did you do to motivate them and nudge them towards their greatness? Someone did that for me over 15 years ago, and I am eternally grateful to her.

How many books have you read that say "HR is not for the faint at heart" or "If you are getting into HR because you love people, think again" well, this is not that kind of book!

The Human Resources profession can be challenging as much as it can be rewarding, and it is in those times, you feel you're proudest to be a part of something bigger than you.

HR is about creating moments that matter to the people around you in your organization and outside your organization. I had a manager who told me I bring the "Kum ba yah," and you know what? I am ok with that because sometimes you need to be the calming force in the storm of chaos surrounding you daily.

I am aware of the reputational damage in our profession, as is the case in many other disciplines. Still, I feel compelled to make a difference, stand tall, and show you what HR done the right way looks like and how you can burst into the greatness within you.

This book is for all of you brilliant HR Pros in the trenches every day, trying to keep your organization together. I said it because it is true; we are the glue, we are the cornerstone, we are the binding agent that keeps people coming back every day if we are doing our job right. I see all of you out there every single day trying to make a difference.

To those of you making us look bad, this book is for you as well because I hope that as you read these stories, you will want to switch vehicles and do right by the people you have a responsibility for, or you will realize it is time for you to move on and let someone who wants to do better take the wheel.

Lastly, I wrote this book for all of you aspiring professionals, studying hard and figuring out how to get into HR. What are you getting yourselves in? I am about to tell you. Sit tight and enjoy the ride.

I wanted to share some stories about experiences I have had as an HR professional throughout my career. The highs and lows of me and why I am still here, and I hope that you enjoy the experiences of my incredible co-writers as well.

There was a time when I felt so alone in my profession and my desire to adopt a more human-centric approach to practising HR. Over the years, I have realized that I am not alone, and there are people just like me who want to bring their human to work and help the people in their organizations do the same.

Organizations driven to put people over process with vulnerability and transparency will always win. So what do you say, will you join the "rebelution"? I hope these confessions will inspire you too.

These are our confessions.

CHAPTER 1

Good & Bad Bosses

"They'll be good days and bad days sometimes; just don't let the bad days change your mind."

Good Days & Bad Days ~ PJ Morton

Confessions covered in this chapter:

1. Bad bosses exist, even in HR.
2. Bad leaders will take their personal "ish" out on you.
3. People in leadership do not always want the best for you.
4. Bad leaders will steal your ideas for their own.
5. HR reporting to the CFO is not the best idea.

At some point in our careers, we have all come across a good or a bad boss. It would always be our endeavour to have a great boss in our corner who propels us forward in our career development, teaches us what they know, and is willing to see you for the incredible human being that you are.

Then there are bad bosses. You know them, the ones who take credit for your ideas, cry you down in those moments when you genuinely believe that you have given the task your level best, and even if you have not, they are never willing to provide you with constructive criticism so that you can grow and move on.

John Maxwell said that "leadership is influence." That in itself says that if you are a leader, you have a duty of care to give your best to the people you serve. You have to show up, guide, develop, and coach them through their most challenging situations and applaud them in the moments of triumph.

In this chapter, you will read confessions from HR Pro's who have dealt with good and bad bosses. You will learn their moments of defeat, how they triumphed over them, and then their lessons learned.

I hope you will identify with these good and bad bosses one way or the other.

If you are a good leader, keep on growing and developing yourself. The key to being a successful leader is knowing that you do not know it all, and that you need to hire the right people to help you grow and be vulnerable as you lead your team.

If you identify as a bad boss, I want you to focus on your lousy leadership practices'. Look at the reaction people have to your words; know that you have the power to influence in the right way and steer conversations to a positive outcome.

These are our confessions.

Confession Journal Entry #1

There are good and bad bosses, and I feel blessed to have experienced both! Yes, I said blessed. I say that because while the bad bosses tormented me and kept me up at night, I learned the most from them. They pushed me way outside my comfort zone and kept me on my journey. My first boss out of college was one of those.

I graduated during the "dot com" burst with a Bachelor of Science degree in Management and International Business. I didn't know what I wanted to do, but this degree gave me options, so that's the road I went down. I was determined to get a great job after college, ride off into the sunset, and live happily ever after. Right? Isn't that every college grad's dream? Well, I sent my resume to everyone that would take it. At the time (not to age myself), jobs were posted on Monster.com, CareerBuilder, or the newspaper. Those probably don't sound familiar to anyone searching for jobs today. But, I used those sources to find myself the job of my dreams. I was lucky enough to have two different offers: a financial advisor and a Benefits Call Center Representative. The benefits role was in Boston, MA, in one of the world's most incredible cities, I thought. So, I immediately accepted that role and took the train in on my first day.

Guess what happened? I hated it! My boss, at the time, was about 35 years old and was on a personal mission to find herself. She came in still drunk from partying the night before. There were only three of us in the call centre, including my boss, so there was no hiding it.

Defeat

My colleagues and I came up with some excellent ideas to help with benefits management, and she took these ideas to the Vice President and claimed them as her own. "I've completely ruined my life by making the wrong decision," I told myself as I left work every night. I decided to get out of HR once I got adequate working experience because I wouldn't say I liked it.

Here's what I did. I put my head down and learned as much as I could about benefits. I built connections with the other people on the HR team, including the VP of Benefits. Two months into my tenure in this role, an opportunity came up as an Executive Assistant to the Executive Vice President of HR. I said to myself, "If I want to go somewhere in this company, this is the job I need to get to prove myself to her." So, I applied. Here's the exciting thing. I was not disenfranchised with the company even though my manager and I didn't see eye to eye. There's a saying in the HR world that says, "people leave leaders and not companies" this was so very true in my case.

Triumph

Two months into my tenure with this problematic manager, I applied for a new job within the same company. Of course, people asked me why I wanted to make this move, and I used my vision and drive as my answer instead of throwing my "bad boss" under the bus. And, I got the job! Not only did I get the job, but I was able to keep some of the benefits responsibilities that I had and got to work closely with the board on their stock option program. Because of my drive to learn and grow, I was able to get some administrative access. I remember walking into the elevator one day, and the CEO looked at me and said, "Hi Michelle, how are you doing today?" I was an entry-level employee at a Fortune 500 company, and the CEO knew my name? I felt so excited and knew then that I made the right decision.

I still look back on this experience when I solidified my passion for HR and started on the right path to my HR career.

This new boss was beautiful. What I hated about working in the benefits call centre were all the paperwork and the upset people. She took the time to show me that Human Resources is so much more than paperwork and upset employees. It was then that I adapted a passion for HR, and I reversed my decision to leave the world of HR forever.

Fast forward a few years, I worked for a global company. I had such a great leader. He was so understanding, empowering, and willing to give his team the space to learn. It was a great fit. There were some differences as this was my first "Manager" role. I walked in on my first day, and he showed me my office and said, "Let me know what you need," so he was very hands-off, which was great for me because I like to figure things out and make things my own.

This organization was growing as they were disruptive in their technology. They had a plan to grow five times in 5 years but hit the goal well under five years. I took a look at the organization and said to my manager, "We're going to have a big need for leaders soon. We could go out and hire leaders, or we can grow our leaders from the team we currently have." The leadership pipeline was minimal at this point, as the company I walked into had 50 employees. When I left five years later, we had close to 500 employees.

I recommended that we put together a leadership development program for our High Potential Employees. This program would include classroom training, coaching, and business problem solving, and it would cost about $15,000 per person plus their time invested. He allowed me to run with it and implement it! This program quickly grew legs and became a global leadership program for new leaders. It's one of the things I'm most proud of in my career. My boss let me run with it, asked me the right questions, and helped me push the cause when I needed to; this has helped me gain confidence in my capabilities and form my competence in learning and development.

This company was also very intentional about its CORE VALUES. I took for granted something because they had a great culture across the organization and the globe. When I left this organization, I learned the value of having reliable and integrated core values (but that's another story).

If you ever want to have a seat at the table and learn more about being strategic, running a business, speaking the business language, working closely with or reporting to the CFO can be helpful.

In my next role, I reported to the CFO of the company, and it had its pros and cons. The CFO was high risk-averse, as many CFOs are. I, on the other hand, am overly optimistic. You can guess that this didn't always go so well. We had a good relationship, but I would come to him with an idea and immediately, he would shoot it down. Here I am, coming from a manager that loved my creativity to a boss that wouldn't let me get two words out of my mouth before he told me I was completely off base. It was so frustrating. I had to push so hard to get my ideas across. I also learned here to "prove" my case with financial information.

This has been so valuable for my career. If you can learn how to prove your case financially, you've become a better-rounded HR Professional! In this organization, I knew how important it was to have Core Values, and I pushed both my boss and the CEO to implement Core Values and everything that goes along with it.

I said there were pros and cons to this. The cons were that I lost a lot of my confidence in this role. Because of being shut down every time, I became afraid to go to him. I also tried to avoid him when I could. However, I learned that I had all my ducks in a row when I had to go to him. It set me up for success in my next role.

My final lesson is that all bosses will have different strengths and weaknesses. They will behave differently and have different approaches. They may make you smile, laugh, and feel great or make you cringe all the time. It's what you do with that that paves the road and defines you as an HR Professional.

I sometimes let the bad bosses define me, which impacted my confidence, but I learned that I'm the one who defines me, which helped drive my confidence. I heard someone say once, "The most important voice that you'll ever hear is the one that's inside you." Tell yourself that you're doing great. Take the feedback from the good and bad bosses and throw out the stuff that doesn't apply. I hope you have more good than bad, but if you have a terrible boss, may it be the best learning experience of your life!

Lessons Learned

❖ Never let a bad boss keep you down. Develop positive affirmations to keep you going each day. Try to have an open conversation about how they are making you feel and if things do not improve, escalate your concern. If you are in HR, go higher, but only after your efforts to rectify the situation have failed.

❖ Know your value and worth as an individual and when the going gets tough, be strong enough to call out those behaviours that go against the grain of your core being.

❖ When a lousy boss goes low, take the high road. Remember, hurt people, hurt people. Try to have a conversation that will allow them to feel comfortable sharing their "ish" and then respectfully convince them to get the needed support and not to take it out on you.

❖ Learn the business of the business from Key Stakeholders such as Finance, Operations and Marketing. They will help you to create a compelling business case when putting your ideas forward.

❖ Clearly show the value of your initiative to the business. Showcasing what the business needs or the problem you are solving is crucial to helping the company understands what they do. Not everything has a financial value attached to it.

Endnotes

1. This quote is from John C. Maxwell, *The 21 Irrefutable Laws of Leadership, Thomas Nelson, Inc., 2007, Print, pp. 13*

CHAPTER 2

Let's Get Engaged

"I think I want to marry you."

Marry You ~ Bruno Mars

Confessions covered in this chapter:

1. Employee Engagement is not an "HR thing."
2. HR often gets neglected in the engagement process
3. People leave inflexible companies
4. HR professionals have to advocate for themselves

I love talking about Employee Engagement. Why? Studies show that globally, the average employee engagement levels in organizations is at a staggering low of 15%. Engagement is a global problem, and while some companies are doing this well, many companies are not.

I will never forget the words I read in the book, **Build it The Rebel Playbook for World Class Employee Engagement.** "Treating people better gets better business results. We have disengaged employees because we lie to them; treat them as adversaries, and give them crappy jobs without autonomy, excitement or accountability."

As I write this book, we are deep in the throws of COVID-19, a global pandemic that has thrown the way we work into a complete tailspin. HR constantly gets critiqued about improving engagement in the workforce. Let me share this; Employee Engagement is not an HR thing! While HR may ideate and create ways to engage the workforce, managers and leaders must play an integral role in this process.

Suppose we focus on what Deborah and Elliott, the authors of The Rebel Playbook, have said. In that case, we can safely say that engagement is everyone's business because we are talking about treating people better. Everyone wants better treatment, and everyone does not interact with HR alone, so it, therefore, stands to reason that engagement cannot solely be an "HR thing."

There are times that I have felt very disengaged in my role as an HR Pro. Times when asked to create a program to engage teams with no budget.

When my idea got shot down because it was not the right time or my listening to employees' feedback to create something they actually wanted was considered me using the budget to satisfy "the mob" (*yes, a CEO said that to me*).

While it is great to focus on employee engagement, let us not forget that HR professionals are employees too, and we also need to be treated better. This chapter will consider confessions of HR Pro's who struggled with lack of engagement in the workplace.

These are our confessions.

Confession Journal Entry #2

Defeat

June 2007

A few months before having her first child, an expectant mother took the time to research and develop a flexible work arrangement to present to her manager, hoping for approval after returning from maternity leave. At the time, her company did not have formal work from home or flexible work arrangement policies; the organization was an "in the office, 9-5 each day" type. This woman (we'll call her "M") scheduled time with her boss to share the detailed plan she had created. It showed how she'd be able to consolidate her workweek to 4 days, allowing her to have her 40 hours complete before Friday and to have an extra day home with her new baby.

She was nervous yet excited as she entered her manager's office. He listened to her rehearsed speech, appeared to consider it momentarily, and then kindly let her know that it wouldn't work; she became devastated. She offered to be flexible and asked to understand why it wasn't a possibility. She said she'd try to revise the plan to make it work. Her manager let her know that their organization did not support flexible work arrangements, and besides, her role required her to be onsite. Disheartened, M left her manager's office. She loved her job, her team, and, yes, even her boss. She didn't want to look for another job. She decided she'd just suck it up and make it work for her return after maternity leave.

July 2009

Two years after the birth of her first child, M was due with her second. She had been working her regular 9-5 schedule in the office every day without complaint, yet was hopeful that her organization had become more open to the idea of a flexible work arrangement in the two years since her first proposal. She had spent time updating her original proposal, this time having various members of the HR team reviewing and offering feedback.

This time, she offered several options instead of just the one; she'd be open to working from home 1-2 days a week as well. Like déjà vu, M nervously yet excitedly entered her boss's office with her new and improved proposal. With even less time considering the ask, her manager again informed her that their organization did not support flexible work arrangements.

Still determined, M researched general facts about how flexible work arrangements improved employees' efficiency, engagement, and empowerment. She also had specific points about how her role could benefit from longer hours onsite and how productive her research days would be if she were able to do them from home M was ready to have another conversation.

Despite her best efforts, he didn't budge. M was determined to find a way to make things work. She left her boss's office and set up a time to speak with the Head of HR. At that meeting, the compassionate leader listened with empathy. She let M know that she had put together a thoughtful and creative proposal but that M's boss was right – their organization did not support alternative work arrangements. Once again, crushing M.

Her second child arrived, and when she returned from this maternity leave, she never quite had the same level of engagement at work. She worked hard, valued producing high-quality deliverables, and met her deadlines but never felt fully supported by her manager or the organization. She went from loving her work to counting the hours until she could get home.

Less than two years after returning from her second maternity leave, she received the organization's highest level of distinction on her annual review, an honour awarded to a small percentage of employees each year. M had her best year yet. She was promoted to a leadership role on her team and was well-regarded as a high potential employee in her department and organization.

Two months later, she quit.

In her exit interview, M let her HR rep know she loved the company, loved the team, and even her boss; it was the best job she ever had. The only reason she was leaving was that the organization couldn't give her the flexibility she needed to strike her ideal balance between her career and her family. She predicted that the organization would continue to lose valuable employees if they didn't create flexible work arrangements and policies that supported employees to balance their lives.

Triumph

March 2012

One month after M resigned, her department piloted a work from home policy, where select employees were allowed to work from home one day a week. It was wildly successful.

Lessons Learned

❖ You are your best advocate. When seeking to enhance your organization's engagement processes, show the data, give examples of other companies where implementation has been successful, and show them the consequences of not moving forward.

❖ Regularly communicate change in policy plans and updates with the organization; if M had known a work from home plan was being created for her department, she may not have resigned when she did.

❖ Most employee engagement initiatives are standardized and generic without considering that there are four generations at times working for an organization. Meaning they all have different needs, and this one size fits all approach is no longer enough. Companies spend over 7 billion US dollars globally on employee engagement initiatives, and the engagement figures are at 15%, says it all.

There is no longer a one size fits all approach to employee engagement. Forward-thinking leaders and HR departments will build flexibility into their organization's DNA to allow employees to create their ideal career path, with all its unique twists and turns.

By being more agile in their decision-making process, leaders at every level will quickly respond to their individual team members' needs, creating the best opportunity for engagement and collaboration.

Building empathy with employees will give you a better understanding of where they are in their journey, and ideating and creating relevant and realistic solutions makes a win for everyone.

Endnotes

2. This quote is from Glenn Elliott & Debra Corey *Build it The Rebel Playbook for World Class Employee Engagement, Wiley, 2018, Print, pp. 5.*

CHAPTER 3

The Robotics of Recruitment

"I'm only human after all. Don't put the blame on me."

Human ~ Rag'n'Bone Man

Confessions covered in this chapter:

1. While well-intended, Recruiters do not always give their best.
2. Being in HR and being in recruitment are not the same things.
3. Hiring managers are not always cooperative.
4. HR is <u>not</u> the sole custodian of the recruitment process.

Although the candidate experience remains a high priority for most recruiters, some of us out here continue to play a numbers game.

Throughout my career in HR, my focus has always been to hire right the first time. Hiring right requires considerable time and effort on the recruiter's part, ensuring that the hiring manager has given you the best comprehensive job description of their recruiting role. Remember, you are the recruiter; it is not your job to write the job description. Empower your hiring manager to give you what they need.

I have encountered situations very early in my career where the hiring manager has left the job description up to me, and in my naivety, I have gone ahead and created it and have them sign off. When candidates start to come through, they go, "what kind of candidates are these?" A mistake I never allowed myself to repeat.

I have also experienced times when I have been dead against a hiring manager deciding to hire a candidate who does not meet the criteria. Still, for the sake of meeting the quota, they have dismissed my advice and hired them anyway (*we will talk more about this in chapter 8*). I strongly recommend documenting that this hire has taken place against your advice in instances such as these.

Every experience matters in the recruitment process, the candidate, the hiring manager, and the recruiter. We are constantly dotting I's and crossing T's to ensure that the process runs as smooth as possible yet, we encounter challenges with hiring managers and candidates daily.

In this chapter, you will read the confessions of a new recruiter and her lessons learned. We should endeavour always to be human in our recruitment process, no matter how much technology the company wants us to throw at it. People deserve to know if they were selected and if not, why not—hiring manager's need to be held accountable and need to participate in the feedback loop.

The more robots we add to the process, the more human we need to become.

These are our confessions.

Confession Journal Entry #3

January 2001 to 2005

I was 17, and I had just submitted my choice of subject to study at university. I chose Psychology as I was fascinated by people, what drives them and what makes them tick. What I would go on to do after I graduated, I had no idea. That was until I came across a module at university that completely captivated me.

Fast forward to September 2002, my first year of university and my first encounter with Organizational Psychology – the science of how people think and behave at work. I was hooked. I knew exactly what I wanted to do – use my Psychology background to unpack the differences among individuals to understand better work behaviour and how these differences contribute to productivity, motivation, job satisfaction, well-being, and many others. I was geeked!

I graduated in June 2005, and less than a month later, I was working in the City of London as a young and ambitious HR professional.

Defeat

I was 21 years old, and my mind was like a sponge - I watched, I listened, I asked, I observed, and I put together what would become my guiding framework of what it meant to be an HR professional – the Dos and Don'ts.

Do's	Don'ts
Treat everyone the same way to avoid discrimination claims	HR can't be friends with employees
Create one size fits all HR strategy to treat everyone equally	Mustn't deviate from policy, no matter what
Write a policy for everything and anything to avoid doubts	HR can't show their real feelings
Be loyal to the business; they pay the salaries	

This framework would go on to become my guiding principle for years to come.

Looking back, it becomes clear to me that we inadvertently ended up taking away people's individuality and freedom to be who they are in the desire to treat everyone fairly and equally.

August 2005

I got the job! I got the job! I got the job! My dream job in my dream city. I got the job of Human Resources Consultant with a small boutique consultancy in Bank, London. We won a deal with a big British bank to supply them with contractors in Communications. My job would be to create a pool of about 300 to 400 contractors that the bank could call upon whenever needed. My responsibility is to source, interview, conduct psychometric testing, take references, and write a summary about each to share with the bank.

Because I am new to this, I got paired with a senior recruiter who is here on an interim basis to support this project; his name is Chris.

Chris takes the lead in the interviews while I sit back, listen and take notes. About everything. From the way to greet interviewees to the questions to ask, how to round-off and close.

October 2005

Ok. So Chris told me he wants me to take the lead in an interview while he sits back and observes. He leaves at the end of the month, and he needs to make sure I am capable and confident to continue the interviews and do the brief from the psychometric testing on my own. I am so nervous. The people we are interviewing are senior to me and more to the point - what do I know?!

OMG, I did it! I did my first interview. I read the questions Chris had prepared in advance one by one and wrote everything down diligently. I am so proud of myself.

So I am a few interviews down, and I am feeling good. My nerves are relaxing, and I can have a conversation with a candidate and smile! Instead of doing some robotic question and answer role-play day in and day out, hardly listening and empathizing.

Wow, this is an awakening. I am shocked and ashamed of how unaware I have been treating people like soul-less individuals. I have been so intent on meeting my targets, asking all questions on my paper instead of following the conversation, writing the feedback almost word for word that I have not created enjoyable interviewing experiences. Not for me and not for the candidates. Is this what standardization does?

Triumph

Self-awareness – when we have it, we can turn any defeat into a triumph. Looking back, I cannot help but chuckle at myself because the alternative would be to cry, which wouldn't change anything. I used to collect reams and reams of paper of candidate interviews. Writing almost word for word, afraid I'd miss out on something critical. And I did miss out on something essential, just not what I thought it would be.

Aha Moment #1 - Self-awareness always wins. I realized that I missed out on relationship building, missed out on listening, and missed understanding. I missed out on creating a great interview and candidate experience.

Aha Moment #2 – Standards are reasonable to ensure quality and consistency in interviewing; however, standardization is unacceptable because it strips people from their individuality and humanity.

Providing a great candidate experience is increasingly gaining importance within recruitment as it not only helps to secure talent and shapes an organization's employer branding. Providing a first-class experience to candidates not only helps companies stand out from the crowd but is also the right thing to do.

As Maya Angelou says: "Once you know better, you can do better."

Lessons Learned:

❖ Recruiters who are not their best selves can be considered tools, and average ones at that if you ask me.

❖ As the world of automation and artificial intelligence takes over recruitment, it is even more important for recruiters to demonstrate good character.

What, then, is character and, more importantly, how is it expressed by those in the recruiting profession?

According to research by the Association for Talent Acquisition Professionals[1], a character is the nexus of six attributes. They suggest these six attributes can be interpreted to describe reputable recruiters as well.

They are:
1. Trustworthiness
2. Respect
3. Responsibility
4. Fairness
5. Caring
6. Citizenship

---

[1] https://atapglobal.org/about/

"A recruiter is trustworthy when they are honest and reliable. For example, they can be relied on to tell hiring managers when their requisitions are unrealistic, given the supply of candidates in the market or the salary they are willing to pay.

A recruiter shows respect when they practice the Golden Rule. No matter how busy they may be or how cumbersome their systems and processes, they treat candidates as they would like to be treated with courtesy and dignity.

A recruiter is responsible when they meet their obligations. They not only fill the requisitions they are assigned but ensure they have the skills and knowledge necessary to do so most effectively and efficiently possible.

A recruiter is fair when they balance their obligation to their employer with their commitment to candidates. They do their best to ensure that they are convinced to join their organization and have a reasonable chance to succeed.

A recruiter is caring when they are considerate of the others on their team. They not only work hard to achieve their success, but they also do whatever they can to help their coworkers reach their goals, as well.

A recruiter is a good citizen when they tap all cohorts of the population when sourcing candidates. They refuse to accept or condone the conscious or unconscious, hidden or visible biases of hiring managers and their colleagues on the recruiting team."

Confession Journal Entry #4

May 1998

Defeat

I had recently joined the recruitment team for an airline. I knew nothing of recruitment, but my old supervisor had recommended me for the role, and as it got me out of customer service, I was up for the challenge.

I had gone through training, and, in a union environment, it was pretty straightforward, not much variation. It was an excellent place to start recruitment.

One afternoon, a group of us were standing around talking about some candidates we had recently connected with, minor complaints. One of the other recruiters was complaining about a candidate who couldn't decide on an offer. There were several calls, with lots of questions about the job offer, the job, and the benefits. In frustration, the recruiter said, "It's not my job to talk them into the job!"

And I thought, "But isn't it, though?" I didn't say anything out loud; I only stood there with my thoughts.

I was young and new to the position. Would she have even listened to me? I never did say anything, nor did I even share this story.

A few months later, she transferred to a customer service position. I was still there. What could I do with this information? I knew she wasn't right.

Triumph

I knew it was my job to convince the candidate to accept the job offer from that day. To do that, I would need to know about the job; I would need to articulate the total compensation package and connect with the hiring manager to understand the position I was looking to fill.

Lessons learned

❖ Take the time to build relationships with the hiring managers to gain their trust. Building trust will become the key to your success as a corporate recruiter.

❖ Remember, there's an element of sales to a recruiter role. Our job is different than sales as we aren't trying to get as many people as possible into the role, but find that the right person. In Talent Acquisition, we need to be a little bit sales-y, a little bit of marketing, a little bit of compensation, a few benefits and know a LOT about the organization.

❖ Take the time needed to learn about the company, the hiring manager, and the position. You are working for them, not the candidate. You need to be able to sell the job and the company to your top choice candidate. If you know your role, you can take the candidates who turn you down in stride.

BONUS

Things to Consider

Firstly, interviews are a place of potential vulnerabilities and confront realities; we remove barriers and where personal stories are shared, stories of triumphs and defeats. It is a big deal to people when we ask them about important events in their lives. So the minimum we can do is to honour and respect their vulnerability. If my focus had been on having a conversation and creating a meaningful connection, interviewing senior people wouldn't have mattered to me. Aged or not, first and foremost, we are all humans.

Secondly, candidates expect the same treatment as consumers. The best candidate experience is about creating experiences that feel real, human, and authentic. It's about building personalized relationships, not just processing resumes. The demeanour of an interviewer is as critical as the questions asked.

The best recruiters can naturally transform the recruiting experience from a mere transaction between strangers to meaningful interaction between two people.

Insight tip - If you are a recruiter, cherish this vital role and treat it with respect and honour. Whether an interviewee leaves your interview feeling excellent and positive versus downbeat and embarrassed, it is primarily down to your interaction.

*"I've learned that **people** will **forget** what you said, **people** will **forget** what you did, but **people** will never **forget** how you made them feel."*
~ Maya Angelou

CHAPTER 4

The Future of HR is Agile

"We'd gain a lot of ground cause we'd both give a little. And there ain't no road too long when you meet in the middle."

Meet in the Middle ~ Diamond Rio

Confessions covered in this chapter:

1. Agile principles are not just for people in tech.
2. HR can adopt agile ways of working according to their needs.
3. Agile ways of working can improve your turnaround time on projects.
4. HR should be involved in agile organizational transformation, but often we are left out.

I t was a cold November morning in 2018. I attended the CIPD annual conference in my hometown of Manchester in the Uk when I came across a booth that would forever change my life.

As I got closer, the lady working in the booth looked warm and reassuring as I asked her, "What is Agile HR?" She smiled and started to explain that Agile, first and foremost, is a mindset that helps us to provide products and services to our clients in a shorter time frame than usual. The focus becomes on providing in increments through ideation and experimentation.

I was familiar with the concept because earlier that year, the company I worked for had decided to carry out an Agile transformation with the tech teams. I tasked with the responsibility to find someone to *"teach us Agile"* (lol). So while the concept was not foreign to me, I wanted to learn more about applying Agile ways of working to HR; this began my journey towards completing my Agile HR certification.

Our world has definitely become more complex since that cold November morning in 2018. According to Deloitte's 2021 Human Capital Trends report[2], *"The need for organizations to better understand their workforce is under urgent pressure from unprecedented, once-in-a-lifetime health, economic, and social challenges. The COVID-19 pandemic is raising critical health issues around employee well-being and safety, as well as remote work and alternate workforce arrangements. The*

---

2 https://www2.deloitte.com/us/en/insights/focus/human-capital-trends.html

pandemic's economic fallout is forcing employers to make tough decisions about staffing levels, worker and team redeployment, and worker retention. And a dramatically intensified focus on social and racial injustice in the United States—and its widening ripple effect—is drawing significant attention to companies' diversity, equity, and inclusion (DE&I) efforts and results."

The success of any business now greatly depends on how quickly we can work with our operations teams to develop robust strategies to create purposeful work that engages and helps people feel connected to the organization despite the challenges we face.

In this chapter, we will take a journey into the world of Agile HR and learn the defeats and triumphs at implementing Agile HR into an organizational framework.

These are our confessions.

Confession journal entry #5

Defeat

I worked for a company that used this model, called the Waterfall model, and employees were working on software for over four years before seeing a result. Lack of results, as you can imagine, was not very motivating. They never saw their work completed, never got feedback, and never celebrated wins. For millennial's, this is a nightmare, and they feel like they're running in a hamster wheel.

We started talking about using Agile across the company. When I began to dive into this, I couldn't fathom using Agile in the Human Resources function. A lot of our work is reactive, especially with employee relations. So, how do you focus on the minimum viable product (MVP) with these types of things? You can't put employee complaints on the "backlog."

The beginning of my Agile HR journey started with failure or struggle. When we started on this journey to become more agile across the organization, I didn't know where to start. I had many frustrating conversations with some of our leaders because we weren't moving fast enough, and we spent a lot of time setting the foundation. Even though it was frustrating, it was essential to help us get buy-in and move forward.

Triumph

I was determined, though, to implement these principles of Agile in my team. We started first with the programs or projects that were redundant and partnered with the business. We looked at the Recruitment Process and implemented a daily standup. We had one meeting daily with hiring managers for all open roles. We gave updates on the recruitment status for that role and asked for feedback on any interviewed candidates that day. We also had a weekly standup with members from other teams in addition to the entire HR team. We invited a member from IT and Quality to prepare them for any hires close to the new hire's help plan, including their space and computer.

Including these team members was a huge time saver and allowed us to move quickly and improved our time to fill positions considerably as we were not waiting several days for feedback and next steps on candidates. It also gave the recruiter the rest of the day to focus on recruiting instead of chasing managers down for information. We could get everyone on the same page in 15 minutes a day instead of sharing the same information over and over to many different people. Our CEO joined the meeting and was updated as well. We also improved our onboarding process with the weekly standup because the HR team and IT team could plan proactively for new hires and their needs.

Standups became a precious tool for the team. We implemented a daily standup as well for the HR team. Again, it was only 15 minutes. Each person talked about what they accomplished the day before and what they were focused on today. We also shared any essential updates, barriers, and decisions made in the previous day, which helped improve productivity and communication across the team. It also ensured that we were all focused on the highest priority items first.

We used a tool called Monday.com to help prioritize our work and give visibility to what the team was working on. We also met weekly to reprioritize work and plan for the next week. As an organization, we implemented blackout times for meetings and planning, so we used them to work on the most important things and be intentional. Every Friday, between 2:00 pm and 3:00 pm, employees were to abstain from email, chat, slack, etc., so everyone can plan for the following week. There was the same blackout rule from 12:00 pm to 5:00 pm to work on their most significant projects and highest priority items on Mondays, allowing our team to focus instead of continuous firefighting.

Focussing on continuous improvement had the most significant impact on our team. As you know, HR can be very archaic, still using paper across the organization. We looked at our processes and technology to figure out how to further streamline our processes, propelling our digital transformation.

We began by moving our physical files to electronic files and changed our performance management documents for electronic forms, allowing us to have more manager self-service, with less filing demands, so the team could focus on supporting the business goals and results.

Lessons Learned

I learned that I didn't have to do it alone. I knew what Agile was all about as I tried to implement it across the organization and my team. It was scary. I reached out to leaders across the organization that had gone through this before and leaned on them. I created a task force and had them help me drive this forward. I had to fail a bit before I figured this out.

Agile is not a one size fits all methodology. Some people use pieces of it; some use all of it. It has to fit and work with your culture and your organization, but it is a change management program. It takes time, practice, and commitment from everyone across the organization. You can't just wake up and be Agile. You will misstep, and you will make mistakes, but it's all part of the journey. Starting with your team is an excellent way to get started. It's a safe place, and you can talk about the successes your team had by implementing agile.

CHAPTER 5

The Company That Learns Together

"A family that prays together will stay together."

A Family That Prays Together ~ Tyler Perry

Confessions covered in this chapter

1. Not every organization sees the benefit of developing its HR team.
2. Over time you will neglect your personal and professional development to prioritize the needs of the business.
3. HR is not seen as a profit-based department and therefore does not receive the same respect as other departments regarding learning and development.
4. Sometimes you have to fight for your development.

H R has been the custodian of learning and development for a very long time. As the future of work continues to shift, so has the responsibility for learning and development. We now see that teams are forming to focus solely on learning and development and a shift in focus to creating "Learning Organization's" where leaders are more accountable for developing their teams. There is a process of unlearning and relearning taking place to create relevant up to date plans and strategies to increase ROI.

Progressive organizations allow employees to focus on their personal and professional development while creating robust training plans attached to their performance plan. As we focus on bringing expert advice to the table, organizations recognize that no one is really an expert, but we are all in a constant learning state, yet HR often gets left behind in this process.

When was the last time you learned something to develop your HR competency besides your degree or certification that got you the job? How did you feel after you engaged in that training? Were you able to immediately apply what you learned to your role? Did it make you feel better prepared to take your seat at the table and own it?

HR is responsible for seeing the growth and development of the people in the organization, including HR, developing itself, correct? Often we neglect our personal development because of budget and other organizational priorities.

As we enter the 4th industrial revolution, how prepared are you to take on the roles future HR roles such as:

- Head of Gig Talent Acquisition
- Head of WFH Development
- Climate Change Analyst
- Director of Wellness
- Head of Organizational Engineering

The balls we are juggling are going to get larger and larger, are you prepared? In this chapter, we will discuss the defeats and triumphs that come with advocating for our professional development and how you can be successful in your role as a learning and development professional.

These are our confessions.

Confession Journal Entry #6

December 2016

Defeat

Have you ever seen a course that you wanted to take, prepared the proposal or request to be approved, only to have it rejected? That's what happened to me. I have always been passionate about my personal development. I listen to TED Talks, read journals and newsletters about all of the cutting edge practices happening in the HR and business space, but sometimes, you need to pay for some types of development.

I am also a firm believer in community because, through community, you too learn and grow. This year, I wanted to attend an HR conference off-island. I prepared my travel request, highlighting all of the talks I wanted to participate in and where I could see the immediate value add to my role and, by extension, the business. When I submitted my request to the finance team for approval, it was rejected. The reason, there was no learning budget for HR.

I was new to the role and had come from an organization where there were always opportunities for HR to learn and grow. So when the accountant said that HR did not have a learning budget, I was in complete shock, especially since I had negotiated bi-annual attendance to this conference in my contract.

How would I turn this around? The response came back that I should pay for it myself if I wanted to attend. At that moment, I began to question my decision to work for this organization. Had I made a wrong decision? Or was this just a one-off situation? I would soon learn that the CEO had little to no respect for HR, and so my professional development seemed to be placed on the back burner unless I did something about it.

Triumph:

In time we hired a new CFO who had a more structured approach to budgeting. He allocated budgets for each team lead in the organization, including HR, which allowed me to attend the conference the following year. I learned so much during those three days and implemented most of what I learned in my role within two months.

One example of this was regarding the recruitment process. I had struggled to find talent in the analytics space, and at the conference, I found out that this was a general concern for most companies. Suggestions were given regarding changing where to look for such talent, and strategies were shared on approaching candidates to negotiate offers. The sense of fulfilment at that moment was indescribable.

I ensured that going forward, the learning budget for my team was thorough down to the ROI and submitted on time as requested and that everything tied back into the performance appraisal for everyone.

The future of work will demand that we step up our game as HR and TA professionals. We need to ensure that we are continuing to develop our HR muscle to continue to add value.

Lessons Learned:

❖ Always ask about the organizations take on personal and professional development during the interview. Ensure that the company you are working for sees the value in developing HR.

❖ Incorporate learning something new into your daily routine. Listen to a podcast, watch a TED Talk, read a book, look out for recent industry trends do not limit yourself. Your learning does not stop with college and university. Our industry is dynamic and constantly changing.

❖ Try to include attending a conference in your annual development plan. Build a community you can learn from.

❖ Always write a robust business case for training, show how the company will benefit from your new-found knowledge and when.

Confession Journal Entry #7

April 17, 2014

Defeat

Of the few stars that I felt aligned against me when I first started teaching the Disc personality assessment in a former corporate HR role, two, in particular, seemed to demand the majority of my attention.

The Imposter Syndrome (something that I can only now name) regularly threatened to defuse any amount of confidence that I seemed to muster.

Additionally, one especially unwelcome voice in my head kept returning to a George Bernard Shaw quotation that I had heard years before and against which I still struggle to this day: "Those who can, do; those who can't, teach."

Essentially, it's easier and perhaps preferable to teach others to do something that you're incapable of doing or unwilling to do yourself.

Although I could certainly imagine scenarios where those words might be reasonably accurate, I feared the possibility of being exposed as an HR pro who mastered the theory but failed the practice.

And then it happened.

A few months later, I took on the "resident DiSC expert" role for my company. One of our regional directors of operations told me that his cursor hovered instinctively over the "delete" button in Microsoft Outlook every time he saw an email come in from me.

As someone who preferred the "D" or Dominant style of behaviour, he looked for emails to be bulleted and succinct. I knew this about him, yet every email I sent this man defaulted to the style of written communication that came naturally to *me* – lengthy and detailed – rather than what I knew he would prefer.

One of the things that I've always enjoyed most about DiSC is that it gives us a common language for considering "cognitive diversity," the variety of ways individuals and teams approach relationships and work.

Yet here I was, entirely comfortable *teaching* these vital concepts and incapable of *practising* what I so passionately preached.

I felt like a failure, and the Imposter Syndrome loomed largely.

Triumph

In April of 2014, approximately eight years after I began working with DiSC, one of our business leaders in Florida requested that I fly down to facilitate a workshop for his management team.

When a request like that came through, it often meant a specific opportunity to address a deficiency in communication, trust, engagement, leadership, or other concern that could negatively impact the operation.

As I recall, this particular visit was simply an additional investment in a high-profile team that was already performing at a high level and looking to get even better.

By now, I had mostly gotten over the initial sting of feeling as though I failed as a budding talent development practitioner. However, I still craved an opportunity to demonstrate my competence.

Before starting this particular workshop, I made a point to meet every attendee, knowing that it would help me remember names and titles for the session to come.

One by one, I shook hands, repeated names aloud to increase my chances of recalling them later, and thanked people for attending.

As I had learned to do, I also paid close attention to each person's verbal and non-verbal communication styles, knowing that I could incorporate those observations into the discussion to come.

I hadn't even gotten to Josh before his colleagues began playing his cards.

"Talk about competitive," they laughed. "You don't want to get in Josh's way!"

The workshop had yet to start, and people were already guessing at his DiSC style. The enthusiastic consensus was that he must prefer the "D" or Dominance style, which is very direct, decisive, and prone to competition.

Intrigued by this sudden focus on Josh, I turned to shake his hand.

"Word on the street is that you're competitive," I joked.

"It's true," Josh responded. "Even if I've never done something before, I *have* to win at it."

(As an aside, other people who prefer the D style of behaviour tell me that it's less about having to *win* and more about never *losing*.)

The slight grin on his face meant for his animated teammates. His eyes, however, let me know that I was learning something that defined him to his core.

Sure enough, Josh's preferred DiSC style ended up being precise as his friends had diagnosed, indicating that he prioritized taking decisive action, making notable progress, and doing those things more quickly and successfully than others.

Following a lively, enlightening DiSC conversation, the team invited me to participate in a 5k run that they had entered. The team was very welcoming, which allowed me to build genuine rapport with the stakeholders I would continue to serve well beyond my Florida visit.

If it hadn't been previously clear that this group got along incredibly well, it indeed became apparent that evening. There was a sense of camaraderie and mutual support that you often find among high-performing teams. They liked each other, and more importantly, they respected each other. How promising, I thought.

I wouldn't describe myself as an incredibly competitive person unless a chip on my race bib threatens to announce my performance to the world.

Without the chip, this would have been a fun way to experience my first leisurely race outside Chicago. With the chip, there were bragging rights on the line.

You can imagine my plight then, when, not far from the finish line, I (second only among our immediate group of racers) came upon the heels of... guess who... Mr. Competitive himself.

I had a critical decision to make.

Do I pass Josh, crossing the finish line first among our immediate team, and pack those bragging rights into my carry-on for the triumphant flight back to Chicago... or do I remain on Josh's heels through the end of the race?

Some of you reading this will be conflicted, even disappointed, by my decision.

Others will appreciate the outcome, perhaps on many levels.

Josh crossed the finish line before me, turned around, gave me a high-five, and waited for everyone else to join us.

Lessons Learned:

Was I in Florida to win a race?

No. I was there to facilitate learning and strengthen relationships with those whom I served. I was there to demonstrate, in this case by example, the power of adapting to connect more meaningfully and productively with diverse personality styles.

Had I passed Josh in those final moments, I would've been saying to him, in effect, "You've told me what you value, what you need from me... and I don't care."

I *did* care, though, and we continued building upon our relationship in the years that followed – something that may not have been possible had I made a different choice during my visit.

What's more, I proved once again to myself that I could indeed walk (or, in this case, run) my talk.

Yes, I could bring theory to life in facilitation, but I was also capable of putting into practice in my own life the very tips and strategies that I was teaching to others.
It felt good.

BONUS

Things to Consider:

❖ What script are you lending the voice inside your head?

❖ How receptive are you to constructive feedback from others?

❖ How confident are you in the unique value that you bring to your work and relationships?

❖ What is your relationship with the space *beyond* the well-defined edges of your comfort zone?

❖ How willing are you to exchange vulnerability for growth and perspective?

❖ How do individuals and teams benefit from embracing cognitive diversity?

❖ How does the world respond when you begin to treat others how *they* would like to be treated?

CHAPTER 6

Addressing the Elephant in the Room

Diversity, Equality & Inclusion - (DE&I)

"Don't decoy, avoid or make void the topic."

Let's Talk About Sex ~ Salt-N-Pepper

Confessions covered in this chapter:

1. There is not enough diversity, equity or inclusion (DE&I) in HR.
2. HR needs to lead by example as we forge ahead with creating diverse and inclusive teams.
3. It does bother us when we see people who are not doing their jobs effectively making more money than us.
4. DE&I is not just about race.

I am a curvy mother of three children, and I am a person of colour. I will repeat this for the people in the back; I am a black, curvy woman with three children. The colour of my skin and my number of dependents is only a part of the sum that makes up who I am as a human being. I am a professional, and I believe that the best person should get the job, regardless of race, age, religion, sexual orientation, or disability. Do we pay for productivity or the biases we create?

There have been moments during my job hunting days where I knew I did not make the cut because of my colour, size, and whatever makes you think that my abilities to do the job would be due to the sum of those things. I knew it from the moment I entered the conference room for the interview.

During "lockdown" going through the pandemic in 2020, I had the privilege of meeting some great HR Pros via Zoom, of course. We had so many conversations around Diversity Equity & Inclusion (DE&I) and how we can do better as HR to make the workplace more inclusive. Sometimes I was the only black person on those calls, and for some reason, I felt no discomfort whatsoever in sharing my story. My thoughts on this topic always start with; if we want the organization to be inclusive, HR must be inclusive. We must lead by example. Not by recruiting token employees to tick a box. Look inside our teams and ask who is missing and fill that space.

I was born in Manchester, UK, to a Jamaican father and a Bajan mother, which I say makes me a "BritBaJam." My first encounter with racism was at the age of 12 when a white girl in my neighbourhood told me that I could not walk to the bus stop on the same side of the road as her. Going to the same school with the bus stop being on her side of the street was a problem. That evening I told my mother what happened. She took my hand and stormed across the road into the house where the young girl lived and approached her mother and told her that if her daughter ever told me not to cross the street to get to the bus stop to go to school again, they would be having a different conversation the next time. My mum is forever my hero for that and so much more.

She moved to the UK from Barbados at the age of 18, and her first experience with racism was on the job where a white woman told her that she heard that black people had tails and asked my mother to show her hers. Not inclusive behaviour for the workplace, and back in the 70's HR was pushing paper.

My grandmother moved from Barbados to the UK to build a life in preparation for the day she would send for her daughters from Barbados. She took her first job as a nurse during the "Wind Rush" period. Her first encounter with racism was on the job when a white patient threw urine on her and called her a "black sambo." Moments that happened in the workplace with no DE&I representative to talk to about what had transpired, and HR was just out of the way pushing paper.

What does the workplace look like today? We have made improvements by talking about DE&I but have we progressed? Let's go back to that Zoom call I talked about earlier, one of the things that a participant said was that she kept silent when her clients in leadership positions made racial comments. In retrospect, she now recognizes that her silence was a way of being complicit in destructive behaviour. Powerful right?

I have also seen persons of colour share their stories about being hired as token employees, with leaders later confessing to filling a quota. We need to take DE&I seriously. Treating it as a ticking the box exercise is unacceptable; we need to do better.

I know that I have focused on racism, and I can hear you say, Julie, race is not the only issue in DE&I, and you are correct. Diversity, Equity and Inclusion in the workplace means more than just ticking boxes to "please the Black people." We are putting the best people for the job in the job, period. People go to school, college, university in all shades and colours, shapes, and sizes. They get the same education, and they come into the job market with the same knowledge and skills.

The 2020 Gender pay gap reports by Payscale [3]shows pay gaps in gender, race, opportunity, education, and occupation. The numbers are too astronomical to digest in one bite; this is an essential DE&I issue. There is still a strong belief that persons with disabilities cannot perform C-Suite functions. Why is that?

Why are there more men sitting on boards than women, and why are they mostly the same colour? Why are there more male CEOs of fortune

---

[3] https://www.payscale.com/data/gender-pay-gap

500 companies than female CEOs? Why are there more men leading educational institutions than females? These questions are proof positive that we still have a lot of work to do.

I have always struggled with the lack of education on culture in organizations. We do not all come from the same background, yet we work together daily, not understanding why we all do and say things without a genuine appreciation for the diverse cultures we have brought together to achieve a goal.

The average number of unemployed neurodiverse talent in the US is 80%, three times higher than their national unemployment average, and the same is true for most countries around the world. Now, that is a lack of diversity if I have ever seen one.

As we continue to wrestle with this global pandemic, we have had a moment to step back and look at this topic of DE&I to see how we all can do better and be better as a human race, in and outside of the workplace. HR, it starts with you.

These are our confessions.

Confession Journal Entry #8

May 13, 2014

Defeat

In 2014, while still building my HR career, I met one of the biggest DEI challenges to date. On a summer afternoon, my HR Manager called me into his office and said, "We have an employee that is transitioning from female to male; we need to put a plan in place to help her... I mean him through this and communicate it to staff." Our staff complement was over 300 people at the time.

I could tell at the time he was flustered, and being honest, so was I. This was a long term employee of the company, and I started thinking about addressing this person. How will we make them feel included? What about the other staff? It was a multi-cultural group; will they be ready for this change? What if we say the wrong things?

While the HR department started putting together a plan, the employee transitioning had started changing physically quicker than expected, and other employees noticed. Over time, the employee started reporting exclusion and inappropriate questions and jokes and harassment from a few employees. While we handled these individual complaints by reinforcing our harassment policies and discipline, we also knew we waited too long to act, communicate and be open with the staff, and we had to own that.

Triumph

Overnight, we went from an "inclusive" workplace to a workplace that would have to prove and reflect how inclusive we were. Over the next couple of weeks, the HR department worked with the employee transitioning to put together an all-staff announcement and a long-term communication plan. Several resources that employees could read about the LGBTQA+ community and the transgender journeys of others.

The employee delivered the announcement himself to his peers; it was deeply personal, vulnerable, brave, and emotional, and amongst many things, he asked that his peers give him time, respect and call him by his new name. My job as the HR professional was to hold space for him, support him, celebrate him, and help all his peers get to a place of respect, support, and acknowledgement.

After his announcement, employees had questions for him and later in confidence questions for me. Some were not supportive because of cultural, religious, or personal beliefs, and they had to grapple with that fact, and so did I. It was a role to support them and work with them to come to a place of shared understanding.

Over the next year, the employee fully transitioned to a male, a couple of employees were let go due to ongoing harassment. However, most of his peers adjusted, used the correct pronouns and embraced him for his authentic self.

Lessons Learned

This year, I started my journey with DEI; previous to this, I knew diversity, equity, and inclusion was important, but I didn't have the lived experience... or so I thought. As a woman, an immigrant, a person whose English was not their first language, I realized, sometimes I was the diverse person in the room. My passion for inclusion started growing then, and I wanted to make a more significant impact.

Equity and inclusion are crucial to employee fulfilment at work. Without these, you won't have genuinely fulfilled employees because they won't feel heard and valued for who they are, and pretending to be someone we're not just to fit in at work is a disservice to who we are as unique human beings.

I learned several important lessons from this story of defeat and triumph. The first one is that it's essential to learn and become aware of our own biases to identify them when they come up and eliminate them when we decide at work. The second lesson I learned was to meet people where they are; you're not going to shift an entire belief system with education and training at work; ingrained beliefs are personal and take time to shift; it takes deep self-work and self-reflection. You have to meet people where they are and try to understand why they believe what they believe and how you can find common ground.

Things to consider:

❖ Measure, monitor, and then take action. You have to measure your organizational diversity and the level of inclusion felt by employees. You can't fix what you don't know, and numbers and scores can sometimes be hard to look at but necessary. Take action from a place of understanding instead of making assumptions.

❖ Educate yourself and your employees on various issues that affect diversity, equity, and inclusion in the workplace; while providing a safe space for employees to learn about others different from them. Only when people feel they can be their authentic self, can you say that you have an inclusive work environment.

❖ Inclusion should not be one person's job, certainly not HR's job. Inclusion should be a part of the organization's fabric; it should be part of the culture and values that drive the organization; it is everyone's responsibility, from the CEO to the new employee that just walked through the door.

CHAPTER 7

Let's Talk About Mental Health

"(Help!) I need somebody

(Help!) Not just anybody

(Help!) You know I need someone

(Help!)."

Help ~ The Beatles

Confessions covered in this chapter:

1. HR professionals are also employees, and we too struggle with our mental health
2. HR professionals are burning out because we keep giving from an empty cup
3. Brace yourself to experience all kinds of trauma in HR, including vicarious trauma
4. HR professionals often neglect our self-care, and we need to do better

Mental health carries a lot of stigma in the workplace; sometimes we see it in the language we use, "she's acting crazy," sometimes in the actions of our managers, "there's no crying at work." In our policies ", you qualify for sick days if you have a doctor's note or you're physically sick."

As HR professionals, we have been told not to show weakness and never let people know we are human. I guess that is why many people believe we are robots. However, circumstances dictate a lot of what we show. Do we ever bring our entire human to work? Some of us do, but most of us do not.

Leaders are supposed to see us as the stalwarts, reliable and trustworthy, ready to act on their every word. We believe our peers will think less of us if we admit for one moment that all is not well, and yet there are days when all is not well.

I struggled with my mental health for a long time, and I know that I am not alone. I know that most of you reading this have had struggles too. If you think for a moment that entering the HR profession means a life of ease, think again. It will forever change you.

When people say, "HR only cares about the company", that does something to me because you do not know the company shame and guilt we are holding. When you say "HR fired me", trust that it was not us that fired you, and if we disagreed with your termination, it could very well mean we did it under duress. We wear scars, and we wear them well.

Every day there is something that has the potential to cause us trauma. Vicarious trauma [4]is a process of change resulting from empathetic engagement with trauma survivors. Trauma is something that HR professionals experience more often than we realize.

An employee is experiencing domestic violence, employees fighting with each other, managers making bad choices, expecting you to act on them, to losing an employee in death. I know that I have barely scratched the surface, but the first time I lost an employee on my watch changed my life forever.

When an employee dies in service

On October 17, 2014, I lost a colleague and friend. It was one of the worst days ever. First, when we got the call about the accident and his death, we were lost for words as an HR team. Then, I started to recall the weeks and months before his death. It felt as though his life was flashing before my eyes.

---

[4] Vicarious trauma as defined by the British Medical Association:
https://www.bma.org.uk/advice-and-support/your-wellbeing/vicarious-trauma/vicarious-trauma-signs-and-strategies-for-coping

I went back to his first day in the office, how he used to make us laugh, his kindness, and his ability to bring people together, his beautiful family. Yet, in some ways, his death still haunts me.

At that moment, you make a vow never to have a favourite employee again. At that moment, you wonder why good people die. At that moment, you wish you could remember every moment, but you can't.

Dealing with an employee with multiple personalities

My first experience with an employee with multiple personalities was another unforgettable moment–no signs of anything strange during the interview process. During the second month of her probation, I got a call from our local deli. They said that this employee got into a confrontation with some residents in the neighbourhood. When I met with her, she started to refer to herself using another name, saying this other person made her do it.

Despite our best efforts to help and get her help, she resigned. There is a part of me that felt that I failed her because she would not get help. There are several moments like this in my career. No matter what I was dealing with or going through, I would always tell myself that I did everything I could and people will be people. But is that always the case? Is that even true?

Dealing with an employee that is being abused

The first time an employee confessed that her partner was physically abusing her and asked me for help, I was frozen back to when I was still at school, dealing with my abusive, alcoholic stepfather. I made a vow to myself to help anyone that found themselves in a similar situation.

Dealing with an employee that has lost a child

The first time I dealt with an employee that experienced her first miscarriage, I cried almost inconsolably when I got home. I shared my story with her when I lost my second child and remembered the doctor telling me that I would never have children after that. Joshua and Jasmin are true blessings because they followed that loss.

Sometimes, we have to go back to a past pain in our personal lives to help an employee as HR professionals. Unfortunately, while we go through that moment, it can bring up feelings that were never fully healed.

People believe that HR professionals are the worst, but we have stories, wounds and scars that you will never see. We go to bat every day for employees and often, with no one to go to bat for us when the time comes, other than ourselves.

It's hard to do all of this and not have trauma. It's even harder to go through trauma and have no outlet to release all of the pain and hurt we feel.

These are our confessions.

Confession Journal Entry #9

January 13, 2016

Defeat

2016 started great in my professional life. My HR career had taken off. I made a difference in my organization, going above & beyond, and my achievements were being recognized.

Meanwhile, my personal life was slowly falling apart. A relationship I had outgrown was coming to an end; I was putting myself through advanced university courses and maintaining the perfect image of the young, successful, "have it all together" career-driven woman (with the ideal relationship and family, of course).

By mid-2016, I was emotionally exhausted in my professional and personal life; I had decided to leave the damaged relationship I have been living in for many years and start fresh on my own. I was slipping up at work, coming in late, making mistakes, crying in the bathroom, being distant & had developed weekly panic attacks.

The response from my manager at the time was, "we've noticed you're not working as hard; you seem preoccupied." I decided to be vulnerable and talk about what I had been experiencing at home. My manager gave me conditional two weeks off. Upon returning to work, I could see that they expected me to produce at the same level as before as if nothing had happened. My mental health was back to normal after two weeks of "time off to rest and relax."

I realized at that moment saying that you support the mental health of employees and supporting it are two very different things. I also learned what a big part mental wellness plays in employee engagement. After many counselling sessions through the Employee Assistance Program, I gained a few tools to handle my anxiety attacks; I started feeling a bit better and, with time, a bit braver. I also had an "AHA" moment where I realized how much we carry to work with us, and I started to ask myself... Are we unmotivated, or are we suffering in silence? Are our sales down because we no longer care about our job or because our marriages fall apart? Are we preoccupied because our kids are homesick?

When life happens, it happens all around us, I remember thinking at the time that my life had changed so much, yet the outside world looked the same, my colleagues, our office, my manager, the CEO, to them it was business as usual, but not for me.

Triumph

When we talk about employee engagement, what do we mean, and how often do we associate it with employee well-being and mental health? Wanting to make a difference, I set out to find ways to create engagement around this topic by talking about mental wellness at work, talking about real things, not just surface-level office talk.

The solution I found was an annual Mental Health in the Workplace program (the cost $1,000). Armed with my personal story and a well-researched, thought-out value proposition, I pitched it to the leadership team, and they were ready to make the investment and support it. The initiative was rolled out over the next three months, with activities, feeling pins, morning mindfulness moments, and monthly mental wellness exercises.

Lessons Learned

During this challenging time in my life, the lesson I learned changed the trajectory of my career. I no longer looked at the people I worked with as managers, employees, CEOs; they were people, human beings that brought their journeys, struggles, and successes to work with them.

I don't believe that's always the case. Sometimes we get wrapped up in numbers, maximizing resources & budgets, and putting out fires. Yet, we forget this simple fact, people are our most significant treasures and ambassadors, and how we treat them & support them in the best of times and the worst of times will be how they treat us as HR professionals, leaders, and the organization itself.

Things to consider:

❖ Take care of your mental health. Often as HR professionals, we not only carry our emotional baggage, but we also carry other people's, and it's essential to know when to ask for help.

❖ Don't get hung up on rigid HR definitions and theories; get creative, look for outside-the-box solutions to help yourself and your people.

❖ When you're pitching new ideas or strategies, use storytelling to captivate people's attention and follow up with numbers, facts, trends and return on investment. You're more likely to get buy-in this way.

Confession Journal Entry #10

I grew up in a toxic house of fear.

As an unhealed victim of child abuse, I was full of self-loathing, super defensive, a perfectionist, and trying to control situations and people I could not. Worse, like this, I spent much of my thirties responsible for bringing other humans into companies, the humans that would make or break that company!

My parents, for their reasons, are broken. In her effort to keep control over us, my mother had us walking on eggshells and not supporting each other; my father failed to protect us. As children, we lived in constant fear of being in trouble, punished for the most trivial reasons, and fearing the harsh physical and emotional repercussions. This fear went straight into adulthood; it went straight into my places of employment.

Defeat:

Can you imagine what it was like to deliver my annual appraisal?

You would mention a minor infraction, something that held me back, and I would take it so personally and protect myself as I had done from the age of 3. You would either end up on the receiving end of a vile stream of angry words or my extreme emotion, as I suddenly balled my eyes out like a child, neither of which you would be prepared to handle. You weren't to know that my childhood had set me up to have this incredible fear of being in trouble.

Triumph:

Purely by chance, at age 40, I ended up working with Michelle Zelli, a coach who specializes in childhood trauma and Complex PTSD. I was so defensive that I would have self-sabotaged and walked away if I had known I was entering into a healing journey. Thank goodness I didn't, and instead, I found my way from utterly destructive self-hatred to a place of self-love, care, and compassion. I am now living the life I choose to create.

Self-kindness and compassion allow you to see the patterns you run, acknowledge them, and be curious about them. The practice I run due to the fear of being in trouble is hard to kick, but my reaction is very different by being aware of it.

I had a lovely chat with one of the Robot-Proof Recruiter Mastermind people, and she wanted to share some feedback. I immediately thought, "Oh no, what have I done wrong?" but I recognized it, I took a breath, and I told myself to be open and hear what she has to say. What she did say was of great benefit to the other members of her pod and me. How different the outcome would have been if I'd kept my defences up!

I did the work to transform; it wasn't easy, but the reward is that I now feel peaceful and happy. It takes honesty to admit that you need help;

child abusers excel at gaslighting and could have you denying yourself that your trauma is even real.

Thankfully, most readers will not have experienced child abuse, but you will have experienced situations that lead to today's reactions and behaviours.

My values are a direct result of my childhood experiences, and I live and breathe my values through my work; I wouldn't change my past.

Lessons Learned:

As HR professionals, you must be curious about those reactions and behaviours that cause you to deal with situations on the job in a particular way.

Humans are not resources or capital to be placed in pigeonholes; they are far too complicated for that. Your colleagues create their experiences, and their reactions will come straight from the subconscious without a filter.

In the HR profession, though, you are responsible for being the best version of yourself because of the critical role you play in looking after these perfectly imperfect people. If you are unwilling to look at yourself and your reactions and be curious about them and grow, this may not be the profession for you, and that is ok.

These words I share are sure to inspire you to get curious about your actions or reactions because you have chosen to be one of the humans responsible for looking after other humans at your company.

CHAPTER 8

A Good Relationship Gone Bad

Discipline & Terminations

"Breaking up is hard to do."

Breaking up is hard to do ~Neil Sedaka

Confessions covered in this chapter:

1. HR professionals are sitting down every day thinking about terminating employees.
2. HR does not have the absolute power to terminate.
3. Terminations take place even when HR objects.
4. Every person terminated does not deserve to be released, and we have to live with that guilt.

My Mum has always been the disciplinarian in the family. Whenever a spanking had to go down, she was the one to give it. Before the spanking always came the "talk." She would say, "Now Julie, I asked you not to do such and such did I not? my reply "yes, Mummy," "so why did you do it?" and my response was always something clever to which she would respond, "Well I told you if you did what would happen. Then the lashes would come.

Little did I know that I would be uttering this same dialogue many years later to each of my three children before I issued any form of discipline? We must be all on the same page as to why the punishment is coming; for some reason, it makes it less bitter to bear. As I got older, I also grew to appreciate the scripture at Hebrews 12:11[5], which states, "True, no discipline seems for the present to be joyous, but it is painful, yet afterwards, it yields the peaceable fruit of righteousness to those who have been trained by it."

I knew at that moment that my Mum did not enjoy disciplining me, but she had to do it so that I would understand that we need rules as a protection, and my obedience was necessary.

I was in training to become a respectable member of society. I never felt traumatized by the spanking, but I did feel the sting, and as it became etched in my memory, I would make a solemn vow to myself never to be spanked again for the same crime.

---

[5] The New World Translation of the Holy Scriptures

On the other hand, my Dad had a look and four words that worked for him every time "cut your rubbish out." It did not take much from Dad to stop me in my tracks and for me to process the immediate need to straighten up and fly right. His hands looked big, and the thought of those hands spanking me was enough to send a shiver or two down the spine.

If only employees worked that way.

I remember the words of my friend Steve Browne when he said that *"parents need to remember that they are raising future employees."* Those words have stuck with me down to this day; as I give speeches to young people on ethical behaviour in the workplace, I am conscious of the importance of sharing those words with them.

While no discipline is enjoyable, we play an active role in handling these matters as HR professionals. How you respond to a complaint from a manager or an employee says a lot about you. Hiding behind a policy is never the answer. Policies are guides and nothing more.

Great HR leaders learn to operate in the grey, and when it comes to terminations and discipline, there can be a lot of grey.

Always remember that we are dealing with human being first and that the policies created are a guide. Seek to understand before taking sides.

These are my confessions.

Confession Journal Entry #11

While going through a recruitment exercise, the hiring manager on the panel decided to hire a candidate that I knew we would have problems with from the moment I met them. Before you say I created a bias, let me explain. When the candidate entered the office, my assistant greeted the person. Then she called me and begged us to see the candidate straight away because they made her feel uncomfortable by stroking the plant on her desk and asking questions about her hair.

During the interview, the candidate was very arrogant in their answers to the panel, and while that did not sway me because they knew what they were talking about, the erratic shifting in the chair and lack of eye contact were most concerning to me. Was this the best candidate for the job? No, I said it upfront to the hiring managers. But they were desperate to fill the role, and all that mattered to them was that this candidate could do the job. They dismissed my words as quickly as I said them in their response by saying, "yes, the candidate seems weird, but we can handle them, so don't worry, just hire the candidate."

I have no regrets with the note I made on that file, "hired under duress," along with a few other words to show that I was not in support of this hire and they would regret it later down the road. We all would.

Fast forward to many infractions and verbal warnings later, and here we are on the day of the dismissal. The meeting took place in my office with two of the employee's managers. We had the conversation explaining while we appreciate the hard work and efforts, we could not continue the relationship, and today would be their last day.

A coldness struck the employee's eyes that I had never seen before. It shook me at that moment. As the manager escorted them out of the building, I took the deepest breath I had ever taken in my career, and when my colleague returned to the office, I said to him, "this is not over yet."

As I was packing up to leave for the evening, one of the cleaners came into the office and asked me if we had an employee that looked, and he began to describe the employee's appearance. I responded yes, but this person no longer works here. To which the cleaner replied, "the employee is in a ball under the receptionist desk!" "OMG! What!" He repeated his statement. I immediately called the managers present for the termination and asked them if they escorted the now-former employee off the compound, to which they confirmed they had. "So why is this person under the receptionist's desk curled up in a ball?" There was silence because, of course, no one could answer me. There was a hustle to the reception area to which we found another manager standing in shock because someone just came out from underneath the receptionist desk and said, "I am going to kill myself", and ran through the door.

One of the managers ran off to see if he could find the troubled employee. I returned to my office to make some calls, first to the police and second to his next of kin, to see if they could reach him. In the meantime, another manager was calling the employee's cell phone. When the police arrived, they commended us for calling them and took the contact information for the next of kin while they confirmed that they would patrol the area to see if they could find the distressed employee.

Later that night, I received another call from another manager who said he had gone for dinner and was sitting on the boardwalk after an evening stroll. The distressed employee appeared from out of the shadows, clearly still in distress, and asked for help to get home. It was a very distressing situation for everyone, but that is not where this story end.

This employee later formed a cyber-attack on the company, which cost the company hundreds of thousands of dollars and tied them up for months in litigation.

Defeat

In retrospect, I wish I had been more vocal at the point of hire about continuing the recruitment process because this was not the best candidate. Hiring to "fill a seat" can be very costly when you do not hire right the first time, which is a harsh lesson to learn.

While I noted on the file that I disagreed with hiring this employee, I wish I had escalated this further because it was a complete disaster from beginning to end. The time that I spent in disciplinary discussions could have avoided.

Triumph

After this particular experience, my managers gained more respect for my opinions in the recruitment process and never left me out of a hiring decision from that moment forward. While I wish it did not take such a harrowing experience for this to happen, I am glad that they could see the wisdom of what I was saying before.

Managers will always believe that they know best. It is your job to guide them to the best outcome, and that only happens when we intentionally use our voice and heart.

Lessons learned:

❖ Raise concerns with managers the moment you notice them in the recruitment process.

❖ Try to show them the financial repercussions of hiring wrong and lead them to the best hire by using your data effectively.

❖ Create a matrix of the candidates under consideration and allow managers to grade them as you go through the interview process. Doing this will help them get a better perspective of what is happening, and their notes will make for a more robust discussion leading to the best hire.

CHAPTER 9

Foul Ups, Bleeps & Blunders

Making Mistakes in HR

"Never mind my imperfections; this is fact; remember that no mistakes too great to recover and bounce back."

Get Back Up ~ T.I. featuring Chris Brown

Confessions covered in this chapter:

1. HR professionals struggle to embrace failure.
2. Failure makes us overthink everything, and I mean "everything."
3. Failure in HR can end your career.

I recently watched a Disney movie called Timmy Failure. The story of a little boy who attempted to solve neighbourhood crimes along with his sidekick, which happened to be an imaginary polar bear. What intrigued me about this movie was how the character dealt with failure. He would just shrug it off by saying, "mistakes were made."

There are times when I have made mistakes in my HR career that have caused me sleepless nights, anxiety attacks and loss of hair. I kid you not, and I am sure that some of you reading now can recall moments when failure has made you feel super stressed.

That definition of HR we all see floating around social media that says that "HR is the unofficial psychologist, event planner, peacemaker, lawyer, and teacher" is the reality for many of us in this profession.

When you are juggling so many balls, something is bound to go wrong. I am sure at some point something like this has happened to you:

- Misentry of someones 401K information
- Over/underpaying an employee
- Made the wrong job offer to a candidate
- Sent the wrong confidential information to someone
- Forgotten to terminate someone in the system
- Mixed up scheduling for an interview
- Misfiled documents

The above list is not exhaustive, but I think that you get my drift. Whether you are working in a team or as a department of one, mistakes will happen, and how you handle what happens next can make or break you.

This is my confession.

Confession Journal Entry #12

April 2014

Defeat

I was working as an HR Associate for a fortune 500 company. One of my responsibilities was processing the payroll. A responsibility that I did not take lightly. Every month, I would email the staff, reminding them to submit any changes they wanted me to make on or before the 10th of the month.

On this particular day, an employee sent me a request to change his local payment. This employee happened to be one of our high flyers and was very influential in the organization. He replied to his request to me in the email that I sent to everyone. On receiving it, I replied to acknowledge his request and accidentally replied to all.

I did not realize my mistake until my colleague next to me asked me if I replied to all on this particular request. It was at that moment I realized I had messed up. A mistake was made. Have you ever had one of those moments when something you knew how to do most of the time suddenly you did not know how to do it? All of a sudden, I could not remember how to recall an email. I was mortified.

By the time I figured it out, half of the staff had already opened the email, and I was getting calls from our office in London about it. The only damage control I could do at this point was to tell my boss what I had done and apologize to the employee as quickly as possible. I will never forget the look of disappointment on my bosses face. I hated that look. I had seen it on my Mum's face before. It always made me feel like I would prefer a whooping than to live with that look.

While the employee accepted my apology, I knew there would be repercussions. A written warning was placed on my file. That traumatised me because I had never been on the other side of this coin before. For months after that, I would check to triple-check any email I sent regarding this employee before letting it go.

Triumph

It is almost impossible to see the bright side of this story, but there is one. I tend to wear my disappointments on my sleeve. A few weeks after my big mess up were some of the hardest I had ever experienced in my career, to the point that I cried most mornings before coming into the office.

One day an employee came to me and said, "Julie, I see you've been looking down the last couple of weeks. Mistakes will happen, I have made loads in my life as a Trader, some that would have cost more than I would have liked them to, but I am still here. You will get over this."

He then went on to tell me about mistakes made by HR in other locations in the group that impacted him. Then another employee came and shared their stories, then another, and another. Everyone makes mistakes, and while they make you feel terrible at the moment, you will get over them and become better for it. Words that I live by to this day.

I never made a mistake like that again, and I became more detail-oriented in my processes.

Lessons Learned

❖ You are human, and you are going to make mistakes. When you do, own it. Take responsibility and let the person your mistake is going to impact know about it immediately. Your courage to admit and apologize will be a testimony to your integrity.

❖ Change your perspective of this mistake. Once you get over the initial shock of the mistake and have owned up and apologized, start to think about what you learned from it and what steps you will put in place to make sure it does not happen again.

❖ Conduct a retrospective of your mistake by asking yourself the questions, what was I trying to do? What went wrong? When did it go wrong? Why did it go wrong? This will reveal what led to the mistake and highlight what needs to change not to happen again.

❖ Put your lessons learned into practice to not fall back into old habits and repeat the same mistake. Implement a checklist to help you through specific processes if you need to.

❖ Review your progress, check in with yourself to see how the plan you have implemented is working out, and if it needs to be tweaked, make the necessary adjustments.

CHAPTER 10

Find Your Tribe

"You are not alone; I am here with you."

You Are Not Alone ~ Michael Jackson

P eople always ask me how I go about growing my network. I did not always connect with people the way that I do now. It took great courage and strength for me to reach out to people. I am socially awkward, especially at conferences and events. Never mixed much, my focus is on finding a comfortable spot and staying there until it is over. I realise that I am not alone when it comes to networking as an introvert.

In 2018 I decided to become more intentional about connecting with people in my HR community from all around the world. First, I wanted to learn what HR was like around from a global perspective. Second, I needed to understand what made people get into this profession, why they stayed so long. Third, I wanted to learn their hopes and dreams, which is when I started to tap into the power of LinkedIn.

Over the past two years, I have been fortunate to meet some of the most beautiful people in our profession. Some of them are now very dear friends, and I am honoured to have some contribute to this book.

Your community is all around you. All you have to do is look with intention, and you will find them. I have embraced being vulnerable to experience and embrace friendship, and it is the most freeing experience you could ever imagine.

Whether you are a department of one or more, you need external support from time to time, and that is where your community makes a difference. I wanted to share some of the groups that I have had the privilege of being a part of and the people I have thoroughly enjoyed getting to know over the last two years. I challenge you to make that first step. Let your curiosity be your guide, and let down your guard. You will be surprised at the love and support you will receive from these communities that genuinely want to help and support you.

My community is your community

❖ **CaribHR Forum** ~ This community is the creation of Francis and Dale Wade based in Jamaica. This community sits on the MightyNetworks platform, and you can join for free. They accept professionals from all over the world, and you can freely contribute to the forum. In addition, they host monthly interactive webinars, have an active WhatsApp group and host an annual online conference.

❖ **Caribbean Society for HR Professionals (CSHRP)** ~ This group was formed by Rochelle James, also based in Jamaica. CSHRP is home to HR professionals from all around the Caribbean. They host monthly interactive webinars, war rooms, virtual games and movie nights. They also host an annual conference that takes place in the islands across the membership.

❖ **Hacking HR** ~ This community is the brainchild of Enrique Rubio, based in the USA, originally from Venezuela. Enrique started his career as an engineer and transitioned into HR. Hacking HR has chapters all over the world, and they host events often. Hacking HR has an active platform that offers mentorships, learning and development opportunities, and a marketplace for sourcing consultants. They also have a very active Slack channel. With over 70,000 members, you will not lack support in this group.

❖ **DisruptHR** ~ This speaker event series is the creation of Jennifer McClure, Steve Browne and Chris Ostoich. This series has chapters worldwide, and I have the privilege of hosting events in Barbados, Trinidad and Jamaica. If you want to learn about how to positively disrupt the world of work, Disrupt is the place for you.

❖ **HR Girlfriends** ~ Sana' (Rasul) Walker is the Chief Girlfriend of this community, and she is a true advocate for HR professionals. Sana' was a great support to many other members and me during the first lockdown in 2020.

❖ **HR Hotseat** ~ Is the brainchild of Erich Kurschat based in Chicago. HR Hotseat has chapters throughout the US. A great opportunity awaits you to connect with this group of fantastic HR professionals.

❖ **HR Exchange Network** ~ The HR exchange network is a great resource centre with blogs, webinars and more. Be sure to check them out.

This list was not meant to be exhaustive but sets the tone for what awaits you on the other side of your fear. As you seek to connect with other professionals:

❖ **Be intentional** about connecting with each person you bring into your space. Your goal is to get to know them better and learn from them and share, so listen and be present in the conversation.

❖ **Be honest** and openly share your experiences. HR professionals are not always good at sharing, especially industry knowledge and expertise. Engage in more profound conversation people will appreciate it when you are your genuine self; this is how you build trust.

❖ **Don't be afraid** to ask and receive help. I have learned so much from people by asking for help. As HR professionals, we have the tendency to let our pride get in the way, but it is ok not o know it all, so ask for help.

Endnotes:

CaribHR Forum: https://community.caribhrforum.com/

CSHRP: https://cshrpteam.com/about-cshrp/

Hacking HR: https://hackinghr.io/

HR Girlfriends: https://hrgirlfriends.com/

HR Hotseat: https://www.hrhotseat.com/

HR Exchange Network: https://www.hrexchangenetwork.com/

Conclusion

"Mi thank God fi di journey di earnings a jus fi di plus, gratitude is a mus."

Toast - Koffee

W hen I entered the world of HR 15 years ago, I had no idea where this journey would take me. It has been a rollercoaster ride to, say the least. I remember my first day like it was yesterday.

I started my career at a company that never had an HR presence before, and I learned a lot about starting from scratch. I then took on my first role in a Fortune 500 company, and I even dipped my feet in the startup world.

While it has not been all bad, the lessons I have learned have made me the professional I am today. The career of an HR professional can be gratifying, but it does come with challenges. Nothing makes me happier than to see an employee achieve their career goals and thank me for working with them, and I know that most of you feel the same.

Equally, it is hard to see employees struggle with managers not stepping up to the task to support them. I have had my fair share of ups and downs in this profession, and this is what I know for sure:

- True professionals will stay the course. However, we cannot fill from an empty cup, so please get help when you need it. We can be heroes and still ask for help.

- If you have a seat at the table as an HR professional, use it effectively to create great experiences for everyone in the organization. You are the voice of the people; you asked for that seat, now do something great while you are in it.

- HR professionals are not just impact makers. We are "Impact Architects." (*Thanks, Khalilah*) You hold more power than you will ever know; use your talents to create products that will inspire others to develop, grow and thrive.

Our profession may not have the best reputation, and we may not always get the pat on the back that we deserve, but we never give up. We keep on going because people depend on us to support them no matter what.

You will feel battered and bruised most days, and You will feel defeated. On those days and in those moments, remember your why. Why you are here and why you made this choice to serve and ignite people. Focus on the moments that you triumphed and tell yourself that this is just a tiny chapter in the story you call life.

I wear my scars daily, some of them with pride that I stayed the course and stood my ground with a leader or manager on a request that did not make sense. The stories that I have heard from employees going through this life. Some of them are genuinely tragic. Holding space for people can take a lot out of you, but I am glad to do it if it helps them. Self-care after experiencing that vicarious trauma is essential.

The moments when I refused to harden and close my door to people who needed help at the request of a CEO who believed that people processes should be automated and HR should be behind the scenes to point them to the policies. That is not and never will be true HR, nor will it be how I practice HR.

I hope that through these confessions, you will learn that you are not alone in this profession we call HR. The experiences you are having are not uncommon, and if you reach out, you will find people willing to share and support you.

You have the opportunity to be great and to do great things, don't ever give up. Go light up the world.

Bonus Chapter

Agile HR

Introduction

Agility and Agile are two of the most used words in the last 3-5 years, particularly with the advent of a world impacted by ecological, societal, political, and economic shifts exasperated significantly by a pandemic lock-down and reaction.

This chapter will share the answers to some frequently asked questions about applying Agile ways of working to HR while demystifying some myths.

Why agility and why Agile though (and why Agile with a capitalized A)?

In my work experiences - 1985 to now - we've seen mechanical, machine-like programming of people, process, and output be challenged by, notably, digital technological advances in the world. More connectivity, more shifts to knowledge work as automation and machines do the heavy-lifting, and more creativity needed in adapting to changing consumer, supplier, and society needs collide to present us with a sure way to be responsive, more creative, and more experimental in our ways of creating solutions.

'Solutions' is a much-used word in the digital industry where agility has arguably created the *force majeure* that has seen the *Titans of Technology* dominate the commerce world and seen an explosion in apps, platforms.

Connecting nodes, be they (seemingly meaningless) social media apps or powerful productivity and data-mining powerhouses.

And within that agility - many of whom use an agile approach to producing those solutions - has given that industry the seemingly unassailable lead in the league tables of value.

Solutions are what it's all about, and for too long - again, in my view, but many others share one, I believe - HR has not looked at its part in the work schemas as a solution provider. Policies that blanket for misdemeanours unlikely to occur in all but a tiny fraction of the workforce. Learning programs that are 'vanilla' and aimed at nobody in particular. And generic sets of values, job descriptions, and performance measures that struggle to equate to real value add, especially in an adaptive work environment.

It's time to move to solutions, products, and value creation that sees the HR function rise like the oft-maligned technology solutions of the 1990s into the dynamic, iterative, and exponential rise experienced by our professional digital brethren. It's time for Agile in HR and agility in the people profession.

Agility and Agile in the People Profession - what do we mean?

It is essential to create a recognized frame of reference for these words; else, they become part of the corporate world's *confetti'*- pretty but fragile words that blow away in the wisp of the wind.

Agility for HR professionals means:

A stable platform of professionalism is held together by standards and legal needs. Still, it is deployed and 'consumed' by others in a responsive, contextually relevant way to ensure there are benefits to realize, value to create impacts to enhance.

Agile for HR professionals means:

A methodology-like approach to how products and solutions are defined; designed, developed, deployed, and delivered using;

(1) Newly-cast accountable roles specific to that situation;

(2) Worked on in creative and responsive Sprints; open and well-defined backlogs of tasks mapped to create a development and delivery roadmap that is adjusted as new insight comes to the fore following experimental and iterative testing of ideas and potential solutions;

(3) Prototypes and Minimum Viable Products (MVPs) that allow us to test concepts into actual solutions that make a difference;

(4) Retrospectives help us adapt our ideas, work allocation, methods and continuously adjust to some fresh insight we didn't know at the start of the process and only revealed by that process.

(5) Cycles, rituals, and ceremonies help us unlearn predictable and stale methods of working up products and solutions favouring more pace, inclusive, and dynamic approaches to deliver something people want, need and can use to create value.

Instead, it focuses on what might **prevent** more agility and the use of Agile in the People Profession. So consider this the article that unsticks the stuck, unblocks the blocked, and gives confidence to any People Professional interested enough in their future to be more relevant and pioneering than their colleagues could ever believe they could be.

I'm a People Professional; how would I adopt more agility and use more Agile in my work?

Let's start at an individual level; because, in reality, that's where the change begins no matter what change program thinking will tell you about coalitions and burning platforms.

Be more agile in yourself has two elements.

How do I think, and what do I do?

One can change the other, and there is no think first, do next. You can do that, and that can change your thinking. At famed London Business School, Professor Herminia Ibarra has said, '*act your way into a new way of thinking.*

My first recommendation is to look at your work as of **now**. How does it arrive at you? What are your processes for acting on that demand/request?

These requests already form into our backlog. They're tasks. Whether it's a simple ', I know the answer; here it is' email to a more complex piece of research into recruitment trends in a particular geography for a specific skill-set.

How do you manage that backlog?

Top of the email pile first and work your way down? Or by the loudest client? Or by an urgent flag on an email?
Here's how to DO more Agile at an individual level.

Individually Agile.

When using a digital application (like Trello, Asana, MS Planner), list your tasks - with one card or entry per task. For example, if an email requires a contract re-draft, then that's three tasks: 1x research the suggested changes for legal and applicability; 1x redraft the contract; 1x Email to send to the employee copying in the manager.

Each one will take: 10 minutes to do the research; 15 minutes to draft the contract and any necessary updates to the HR Information System; 5 minutes to prepare the email. So 30 minutes in total.

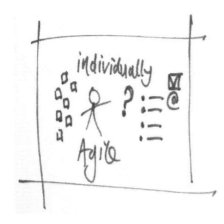

Repeat this exercise for as much as you feel you need to for the day's work or what else is in your backlog.

Start the day and tick off as you go. You could even use the Kanban board method. Three columns. All the tasks to do today, as a day's sprint' in the **To-Do** column.

Pick the one you need to do with the most urgency. Move it to the **Doing** column. ONLY ONE THING AT A TIME, mind.

When you've done that, move that to the DONE column with a sense of appreciation and fulfilment.

And repeat.

One task at a time. Focused, attentive, planned, but adaptive. If something comes in that's urgent during your day: Immediately raise a card/entry for that. Move the thing you were working on in **Doing** back to **To Do.** Move your urgent task into **Doing.** Do it. Move it to **Done.** Then return to your previous 'doing' and move that back to the **Doing** column.

Clear of mind on what work you should be doing. No distracting litany of tasks where concentration can stretch. Focus. Better results. Happier clients.' More satisfaction at the end of the day when you see ALL the tasks in the **Done** column.

And repeat for the next day and so on.

This personally is Agile and showing some personal Agility.

Let's use this to bust a myth or two now.

Myth #1 - Agile and agility means messy and is an excuse to ignore good planning.

As we can see from this example, planning is precisely what an agile approach is all about. To exercise more agility, we need to plan for it. It's not as randomized as some think it is. And while that might sound a bit *oxymoron* to be both planned and Agile, it's precisely the non-fixed type of planning we've all been hoping for. ENOUGH is the word I use a lot. There are **enough** planning and **enough** adaptation and agility.

Agile is the perfect foil for overconfident planning that creates the illusion of control.

OK, so we're mastering individual Agile and, thereby, agility. What next?

Well, not just because you've done this, but let's now look at collective agility and Agile in togetherness working.

Collectively Agile

We must see Agile and agility as *things we do and how we are.* Collective agility and collectively Agile are part of the same equation - doing things better together.

To learn how to use agility and use an agile approach to working, you can start with you, as this piece illustrates. OR you can join in with others and do it together. The same methods are often at play but more accountable to others, so going beyond yourself.

In this version of agility and Agile are some very vital mindsets, approaches, and ceremonies:

1. **Openness and participative**. Not just being an extrovert, but active, inclusive, sharing, and willfully clear about how you are and what you're feeling.

2. **Courageous and compassionate.** Being safe to speak up, challenge, and suggest others doesn't prevent what is known as *radical candour*.

3. **Focused and creative.** We need to plan with tasks, including identifying and logging and planning, estimation, and completion. While this might seem mechanical, all we're doing is creating a fighting chance to tackle our workload and achieve our dream/goal of a solution that matters.

4. **Iterative and responsive.** In this instance, we test our ideas and admit that it got us to the next version or iteration if they don't work as planned. So we lose our ego-based attachment to our opinion and go with what it revealed—something better for the people we are serving with our solution or product.

5. **Reflective and deductive.** In the ceremonies of Agile, retrospectives and Sprint reviews allow us to look back to look ahead and deduce where we - or you - were on fire or misfiring. It's a tough admission to start with, but it's healthier for growth in the long run, and in the future, you will thank yourself for taking it on the chin and learning.

Ultimately, Collective Agile is *learning in the flow of work.* You can study and learn how to do Agile, but you can only become better with agility by doing it. It's team learning of the most practical nature.

Practically, you still follow the rituals of individual Agile with some added elements for collective understanding, appreciation, and clarity:

(1) **Aspiration.** Conduct a solution challenge based on good problem analysis (using the Problem Statement approach can be constructive here).

(2) **Vision.** Have someone set a clear and compelling desire for the future state to ultimately become the owner of the solution to deploy for others' benefit.

(3) **Roles.** A good Product Owner clearly defined who will take the built solution 'to market.' An excellent Agile Coach can help the team be focused, adaptive, cohesive, together, challenging, creative, disciplined, divergent as needed, and help bring in expertise as required, keep the team lean and effective, and help clear blockages revealed. And an excellent agile team - of determined, creative, committed souls who want to build something of value.

(4) **Process.** The formula for Agile is as described in the individual agile approach but with multiple contributions and considerations. Backlogs, Sprint Planning, a Roadmap, development, adaptation, retrospective reviews, adjustments, prototypes and trials, research and evidence-based experimentation, decisions, production, and deployment readiness are all features of an Agile approach. And it wins when

done in the context of the people and the challenges faced in producing that solution.

So either you learn more about the agility of self-first, then venture into collective agility and Agile, or learn in collective agility and Agile frames and adapt yourself as you go and introduce the more suitable to your own routines rituals. It matters not and can be either/and.

Myth #2 - Agile and more agility will only work if we invest heavily, and we simply cannot afford that.

Agile and agility grow gradually. It isn't about an on/off switch to flick.

It's about learning, sensing, adapting, and integrating Agile and agility to live alongside formal, rigid, and traditional approaches for a while or for longer.

It, therefore, should build gradually, and confidence and capability can be enhanced one person, one product or solution, and one program of works at a time.

What is gained in one productive use of Agile might be a 2% quicker and 10% more effective product or solution. The next time that same team tackles a challenge, it might be 20% faster and 50% more effective. So by the second round of Agile, you'll likely have acquired more time, energy, impact, and even capital than you invested. Multiply that by every significant challenge or a new piece of work you undertake, and the gains are consistent and acquire with each wave of an Agile product-based team's efforts.

I assert that you cannot afford NOT to invest in partial or whole scale Agile and agility-based changes to how you work. Friction loss will become calcifying and make work harder than it needs to be. Less friction - using Agile and agility-based approaches - will become the regenerative method for continually improving and forever adapting to change.

Systemically Agile

My advice is NOT to introduce this at first but to build agency, confidence, and capacity at individual and collective levels before reimagining your entire operating system and upgrading it.

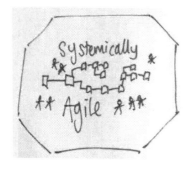

Someone should take ownership of a system-wide introduction of more agility and Agile ways of working. Building on the smaller, connected efforts of collective and individual agility seems a natural next step.

What will surface are challenges and splicing with traditional, less-fluid ways? And to some, this means it will become inefficient or ineffective (or both).

Deliberately paying attention to not just what you are producing but, more so, how you are producing it will become a norm. The agility-based mindset will become more restless in pursuit of each person making marginal gains and more gigantic leaps into more effective and value-creating ways of being, working, and measuring.

This state sees something like the People Profession within an organization enter into being an enterprise. A provider of services and stretch. A supplier of products and experiments for the future. Not an order-taking bureaucrat insight, but a strong force for good in both ethics, kindness, and productivity as a co-existing force.

And Agile and agility are a must in helping us be that.

OK then, how do we do this larger-scale shift? An archetypal plan that may need adaptation considering the context and perspectives held in your organization but typically, it might look like this:

1. **Evidence.** Collective Agile will need to be at play with enough variety and measured success that proves this is a systemic change not only required but undeniable. You'll need evidence in more than speed here. And there should be a rich scorecard based on;

    a. **Human value** - how do people feel working like this?

    b. **Intellectual value** - what have people learned and shared working this way?

    c. **Material value** - what we've created lasts and serves its purpose better this way.

    d. **Social value** - togetherness and candor are increased by working this way and what this delivers is more cohesion and challenge that ensures we don't transact our way through the relationships side of who we are

    e. **Ecological value** - not necessarily of the green-energy type but in the eco-system of work, what this means for a sustainable way to perform and learn.

f. **Financial value** - of course, the ultimate show of gain and thereby prosperity in working this way - what it saves, realizes, and ultimately delivers in monetary terms.

2. **Confidence.** There must be a core group of confident people who believe and sense this is the way to go for a more systemic level of agility and Agile practices. Others become more willing to build their confidence in detaching from conventional ways to be more fluid in planned responsiveness. Will it mean the end for those who don't believe in it or their ability to adapt? Not necessarily. It will be a good chance for some to test themselves, and also, some work may still sit in the 'no need for agility/Agile' so that could find you with a more useful hybrid set up.

3. **Cadence.** A series of rhythms and regularity embeds agility and agile ways so that it becomes habitual. This means more than merely planting new processes though they will be like the musical score that becomes your symphony. Devising approaches to move you to more agile ways and agility of approach will start with agreements and plans and eventually become your new way of operating and being.

To learn more agility and be more Agile at a systems level, you will DO more agility and Agile while testing and responding to what doesn't benefit from that approach.

My agility and Agile story - failing your way into agility.

All of the above comes from my personal experiences, and now, partly what my business exists to do is create more agility and introduce Agile to more of the HR profession.

In helping Julie put together this book, she specifically asked for success stories and failures that somewhat validate my claims and proposition and show others what helps make people who they are.

The starting point.

Agile and agility didn't come to as a packaged 'box of tricks.'

I discovered self-managed organizations and more pioneering and rule-breaking entities. I think it was that I liked more—anarchy over hierarchy. Starting with the usual for most people: Ricardo Semler's Maverick - a book I bought but left on the shelf for a while. And then, through sheer luck, I got to go to a talk by Gary Hamel - now one of the world's most renowned Management Thinkers. In it, he talked about his book **The Future of Management**. The self-managed enterprises enraptured me he spoke about, and that management was a now mostly defunct *technology* of the 20th-century industrial era.

So I got Maverick off the shelf, found articles, movements, and methodologies that were all about self-management. It was 2007, and I became sold on the entire concept.

I then discovered Agile and Scrum as an extension of this approach. And what I found was, self-management was too radical for most, but the tech industry was all over it, bearing in mind we had the early days of Facebook and Google was a search engine only, and there was no Air BnB or Uber.

So I tried to experiment with it in the L&D team I was leading. And here was my first mistake.

I introduced a systemic approach to our work without anyone saying they wanted, needed, or were willing to work in this way.

There wasn't a problem to solve that this was the solution to. I liked the idea, felt it was the progressive thing to do, and set about introducing a more self-managed and agile workflow.

I introduced a system called **The Hub**. A spreadsheet where all our work went. I didn't know about Basecamp and Asana, and Trello did not exist yet.

We toiled away trying to understand how work flowed to and through us, and then from us, and we developed some more robust processes, but we didn't see any 4x speed or 3x quality improvements.
I think the team was amiable and indulged me in something they didn't sense or believe in.

In 2010-11, a vast new CRM and Case Management system was being designed and implemented. We split the team, and through our embedded sub-team, we were working specifically to create the learning as the CRM system's modules were built.

We thought we were working in a responsive, adaptive way following the development of learning modules to match system functionality. In truth, we were simply following a release schedule and more rework on modules negated our 'early advantage' on being iterative.

So we THOUGHT we were Agile, but in respect of the core rituals I now know and love, we were a *bite-size waterfall* operation.

Ultimately, that and a series of big 'clangers' led me to leave that company - suddenly and under a bit of a cloud. I wasn't working how I wanted to be; I compensated for that with more work attempting to show how we could try and be adept and agile in handling a more significant portfolio. And through my poor decision-making, I did some dangerous things. I had to go.

Into freelancing and there was an increased desire to work on things that were of the self-managed and Agile ilk, but in the world of HR, Organization Development, and Change, there wasn't a huge demand. Sure I found communities and already 'converted' organizations that didn't help me be that way. BUT I learned from them.

And as a result, I realized that my failed attempts in the self-managed and agile areas were great learning moments for me. Embedding what I'd experienced by researching and spending time getting to know the individual, collective and systemic components of some of the world's most pioneering yet unheralded companies helped me assemble my version of Agile.

What was significant about that was the crucial realization that Agile has principles, rituals, and elements. Still, the assembly of them and the utilization of them depended on the problem(s) to be solved, the confidence and mindset of the people who could learn their way into being Agile, and the governance, systems, and flow of work and decisions made as to their de facto standards.

I had found an amalgamation of **Agile** (used in Tech Development), **Self-management** (used in progressive systems in pioneering organizations), and **Organization Design and Development** (used already in aspects of HR and Change).

From 2015 through to the present day, I've been adopting these approaches into consultancy as a way of operating as a micro-enterprise. In HR, OD, Learning, and Change teams, Agile has become the *almost* standard offer, tailored, of course, to meet the context of the operating environments in over 40 companies across all sizes and sectors.

One client in local government used the agile approach for their projects and went on to win Digital Council of the Year in 2018. They reported a 4x concept to delivery ratio; more inclusivity, higher engagement levels, more successful projects 'right first time. Agile, iterative development worked so well that their responses to the COVID-19 situation were highly inclusive and incredibly rapid.

Agile and agility work well when embedded into the way things are around here—their words, not mine.

Deloitte's *Human Capital Trends* report in 2017 and 2019 reported that *'Today's high-performing businesses increase their agility and speed to market by re-organizing their employees into networks of small teams.'* Whether using more agility or an agile approach to their work matters not so much. That they are agile is the key finding from this research.

It's a continually adapting approach, but then, being Agile, why would it be anything else?

Introduction To HR@Heart

In September 2019, I experienced my second bout of HR burnout. I was dealing with stress at work and home, and it did not seem as though either situation would ease up anytime soon. I remember my mum taking me to the doctor and bringing me home, and she slept on my couch for four days until I could eat and walk around without looking like I was going to collapse.

At that moment, I asked myself if this career called HR was really worth it. I also started to question if this thing we call life and all the effort it takes to live it. Was I living my life with purpose and intention? Why and how was I pouring into others because I certainly was not refilling my cup sufficiently to support what I was giving out.

Then one day, I was staring at the ocean view from my patio, and I realised that this was not the journey or course my life should be taking. There was a voice inside of me that started to say, time for something new. I began to think about what I loved about HR and what I did not like about HR. The pros outweighed the cons, so I knew that leaving HR was not the answer.

I decided to embark on my journey of discovery, and it was at that moment that I hired my coach. She inspired me in ways I could never have imagined, and through my sessions with her, I created HR@Heart

Consulting Inc., a safe space for HR professionals to lean in, grow and thrive.

I now support my HR community by conducting 1:1 or group coaching sessions, where I take them on a journey of self-discovery to unleash the champion within. If you are feeling lost and alone in your HR career, I am here for you. You are not alone, reach out, ask for help. I got you.

I will equip you with the skills, confidence, and determination to achieve your goals. In addition, I will leave you equipped with the most current approach to your career management.

About The Author

J ulie Turney is a People Experience architect with over 15 years of experience in the Human Resources (HR) profession. Julie built her career from the bottom up and has worked in various industries in established companies, from startups to Fortune 500's, working in cross-functional  teams to support purposeful work and create meaningful cultures.

Julie is the Founder and CEO of HR@Heart Consulting Inc., a boutique coaching firm with a global client base, providing safe spaces for HR professionals to lean in, grow and thrive. A company birthed out of her second bout of HR burnout. Julie found creative ways to heal from her burnout experience and decided to share her coping mechanisms with her hr community, helping them do the same.

Julie is the Host of the HR Sound Off Podcast Show. Created to demystify the many misconceptions people have about the Human Resources Profession, Julie interviews HR professionals across the globe and shares their stories. She hopes to make the profession and the people in it more real to each listener.

Julie also has a passion for technology and seeing future generations develop viable careers in tech across the Caribbean. She works with The Source Code Developer Academy, part of Ten Habitat's non-profit organisation, to create tech careers for people in the Caribbean through strategic partnerships with corporate entities focused on recruiting digital nomads worldwide.

Index

Made in the USA
Middletown, DE
10 January 2022

58329335R00093